Married to the Job:
Wives' Incorporation in Men's Work

Married to the Job: Wives' Incorporation in Men's Work

JANET FINCH

University of Lancaster

London
GEORGE ALLEN & UNWIN
Boston   Sydney

George Allen & Unwin (Publishers) Ltd,
40 Museum Street, London WC1A 1LU, UK

George Allen & Unwin (Publishers) Ltd,
Park Lane, Hemel Hempstead, Herts HP2 4TE, UK

Allen & Unwin, Inc.,
9 Winchester Terrace, Winchester, Mass. 01890, USA

George Allen & Unwin Australia Pty Ltd,
8 Napier Street, North Sydney, NSW 2060, Australia

First published in 1983

British Library Cataloguing in Publication Data

Finch, Janet
 Married to the job.
1. Husbands—Employment 2. Wives
I. Title
305.3′3   HD4901
ISBN 0–04–301149–7

Library of Congress Cataloging in Publication Data

Finch, Janet.
 Married to the job.
Bibliography: p.
Includes index.
1. Wives—Effect of husband's employment on.
I. Title.
HQ759.F47 1983   306.8′72   82–16435
ISBN 0–04–301149–7

Set in 10 on 11 point Times by Wyvern Typesetting Ltd, Bristol
and printed in Great Britain
by Biddles Ltd, Guildford, Surrey

Contents

Acknowledgements

My interest in exploring wives' relationship to men's work, and in trying to develop a sociological analysis of it, began with my Ph.D. thesis on wives of the clergy. I am pleased therefore to begin this list of acknowledgements by registering my gratitude to John Eldridge, whom it was my good fortune to have as supervisor; and also to Sheila Allen, whose department provided a supportive environment for me at that stage, as it has for other women sociologists. Initially John Wakeford, and then David Morgan, encouraged me to embark upon a book on this topic, and both retained an active interest in its progress.

A number of people gave me assistance in collecting material. Janina Brzeskwinski and John Clements helped me with references in their own specialised fields. The officers of the Diplomatic Service Wives' Association helped me to check details of the position of wives in the diplomatic service; and Mr E. Armstrong of the Home Office Prison Department gave me valuable assistance on the details of housing for prison officers. The Soldiers, Sailors and Airmen's Families Association allowed me access to the full set of their magazine. I owe a particular debt of gratitude to Maureen Cain, who generously made available for my use data from her study of police wives, and offered encouragement throughout the writing of this book.

In developing my analysis of wives' incorporation in men's work, I have benefited greatly from participating in seminars and discussions with other academics working on similar topics, especially in the Sexual Divisions study group of the British Sociological Association, and the Lancaster University Women's Research Group. Particular thanks should go to a number of colleagues who have discussed ideas with me on many occasions, especially Mary Ann Elston, Dulcie Groves, Frances Price, Kate Purcell and Helen Roberts; and to several graduate students who certainly have contributed to my work, as I hope I have to theirs, especially Sue Duxbury, Felicity Harrison, Richard Hugman and Emma Redmond Pyle. Especial thanks are due to Sylvia Walby, not only for her continuing encouragement, but also for her perceptive and constructive comments on the final draft of the manuscript. The typing was ably and cheerfully undertaken by Sarah Bracewell.

My thinking on this topic owes much to many conversations with friends, academics and others, who have shared their own experiences of marriage with me. From many women I have learned about the personal, and sometimes painful, consequences of being married to the job. For obvious reasons, I shall not name them here. Some men also have earned my admiration for their attempts to live non-sexist marriages, and I would like to dedicate this book to two of them: for Carl and Dick.

1

Introduction

The Book's Focus

There is a familiar theme in our culture that marriage entails 'taking on' your partner, for better or worse. Marriage is not simply a limited liability contract, but each partner – the theme runs – brings to the marriage their total persona and its consequences, which the other has to respond to, handle and deal with. One feature which has to be taken on board is the spouse's job and its implications. What does it mean to marry a bus driver, a solicitor, or a bank clerk, and is that different from marrying a policeman, a clergyman, or a miner? If so, *how* is it different? The examples are chosen advisedly to indicate male occupations, in the belief that this, like so many other features of marriage, is different for men and women: the implications which a man's paid work has for his wife are more significant and far reaching than vice versa. The central theme of this book is that when a woman marries, she marries not only a man but also she marries his job, and from that point onwards will live out her life in the context of the job which she has married.

This theme – relatively under-explored in sociological literature (Fowlkes, 1980, p. 7) – can be seen as one facet of examining the overlap between work and family. This particular overlap has two important characteristics. First, it focuses on specific jobs rather than 'work' in general. In so doing, some important general issues are raised about the organisation of paid work, but the analysis concentrates on features of specific jobs and the implications which each has for the wives of male workers. Secondly, the implications of men's work are explored in relation to their wives, not 'the family'. This means that women are seen primarily as wives, rather than the (perhaps more usual) focus of women as mothers, although clearly the two cannot be completely separated: the implications of a man's work may be somewhat different for the wife who is also a mother. It is, however, the specific consequences of marriage rather than mother-hood which are explored in this study.

The concentration upon wives does not imply that no one else is affected by men's work. Children, and indeed other adult members of the household, may experience equally significant effects. A parallel study which concentrated upon them would be an interesting but a separate exercise, for the implications are unlikely to be precisely the same as for wives. This book concentrates on the latter, rather than upon all household members, on the grounds that the structural position and cultural meaning of being a wife is likely to shape the effects of men's work into particular forms, and to give them a particular character.

The relationship between a wife and her husband's work is seen in this study as a two-way one: his work both structures her life and elicits her contributions to it. These terms have been selected because they seem to best capture the processes which I wish to identify, but since there is room for misinterpretation, I will specify more precisely what I mean.

The first part of the two-way relationship is that a man's work imposes a set of structures *upon* his wife's life, which consequently constrain her choices about the living of her own life, and set limits upon what is possible for her. Those structures are, of course – both analytically and in experience – part of the more general structure into which, characteristically in our culture, a woman enters when she marries. As Gillespie has put it, 'to fit the master-plan of the other becomes her life's work' (Gillespie, 1972, p. 132). The character and shape of that master-plan varies in different marriages, and, it will be argued, an important part of that variation is accounted for by the jobs which men do. In selecting the word 'structure' for this, there is perhaps a danger of implying a much more deterministic model of explanation than I intend. Certainly I do not wish to suggest that such structures are unchanging or unchangeable, nor that wives merely slot into some pre-ordained role. Indeed, I have argued elsewhere (Spedding, 1975, pp. 470–82) that such interpretations are inadequate even in instances where wives apparently are acting out a conventional stereotype. The problem here is one fundamental to all sociological accounts of social life: how to steer a course between individualistic and deterministic explanations without finally saying nothing at all. The use of the concept of 'structuring' is intended to underline the externality of constraints as wives experience them. That is, largely they are 'givens' (or at least are *accepted* as givens) to be accommodated and worked around, and the patterns which they impose form fundamental organising themes for wives' lives.

The other side of the two-way relationship is that wives contribute *to* the work which men do. Again the character and the scale of these contributions varies significantly with particular jobs. The word 'contributions', which perhaps has a somewhat insipid ring to it, has been selected as a general way of describing this process, because it leaves open certain key questions, especially: How far are wives' contributions enforced or chosen? How far should those contributions be seen as labour which is extracted by husbands, or by capitalist employers, or by both? These are important issues which need to be explored further after the evidence about the character of those contributions has been reviewed.

A wife's relationship to her husband's work is seen therefore as a two-sided coin, whose shape and size varies in relation to men's jobs. The implications for one side cannot simply be read off from the other: those jobs which impose the most rigid structures may not be the same ones which elicit the most direct contributions from wives, and vice versa. The word 'incorporation' is used in this study as a shorthand term to denote both sides of the coin. So a wife's incorporation in her husband's work consists both in her incorporation into the structures around which that work is organised, and the incorporation of her labour into the work done.

Conceptual Starting-Points

This discussion of conceptual starting-points is not intended to provide a comprehensive literature review; rather to specify key sources which I have found useful in raising some initial questions which this study pursues. Those sources are discussed here primarily in relation to the questions which they raise, although they also provide reference points to which the discussion returns later.

The sources are of three types: sociological and related writings on work and family; two specific articles which address wives' incorporation; and several other articles which have raised issues about parts of, rather than the whole, analysis.

The Sociology of Work and Family

This notion of a wife contributing to her husband's work has not been absent entirely from the literature of the sociology of marriage and the family, but it has never been a central interest. For example, Blood's textbook on marriage does mention that wives may be able to advance or hold back their husband's career, but only five sentences are devoted to this issue (Blood, 1969, pp. 222–3). In British sociology, well-known textbooks on the family such as those by Harris (1969) and Farmer (1970) give it no specific mention. In a review of sociological work on a related issue – the relationship between a husband's occupation and his wife's employment – Mortimer, Hall and Hill (1978) identify sociologists' relative neglect of the whole area of wives' involvement in the 'central role elements' of their husbands' work. In more general terms Bott, in her pioneering study of aspects of the relationship between husbands and wives, did raise the issue of how far different forms of conjugal relationships could be related to male occupations, although she does not pursue these links in sufficient detail to make her empirical material useful in this study (Bott, 1957, especially ch. III).

Looking more generally at literature on the family and productive work in capitalist societies, it is clear that work and the family mostly are treated as analytically separate spheres. This observation goes some way to explaining why the issue of wives' incorporation often has been neglected: sociologists of many different theoretical persuasions have rather readily accepted the view that one consequence of industrialisation was the separation of work from the home, creating the public sphere of work, and the private domestic sphere (for example, Farmer, 1970, pp. 12–15; Moss and Fonda, 1980, pp. 8–10; Secombe, 1974, pp. 6–7). Thus, it is assumed, paid work became associated with activities taking place outside the home in separate locations and at specific times. These activities are largely undertaken by men, leaving women to be assigned to the domestic sphere as their particular realm. If one accepts this as the basic analysis, the relationship of wives to men's work does not emerge as an obvious issue, since it traverses the supposedly separate spheres.

The separate 'spheres' view of work and family can be, and has been, challenged on a number of grounds, most importantly from the point of view of this study: that it is empirically insupportable; that it is theoretically naïve; and that, not merely is it not useful as an analytical tool, but it serves actually to obscure certain important features of social life. Davidoff's (1979) interesting article on landladies and lodgers in the nineteenth and twentieth centuries provides one clear challenge on empirical grounds, since the economic and domestic relations displayed by this example do not fit neatly into either the productive or the domestic sphere. Davidoff argues that her examination of the recent past 'should be a reminder that there is no natural or fixed separation between a public and a private sphere' (ibid., p. 93). That view would be shared by Lasch, who calls the presumed isolation of the family from work 'a sham'. 'In reality, the modern world intrudes at every point and obliterates its privacy. The sanctity of the home is a sham in a world dominated by giant corporations and by the apparatus of mass promotion' (Lasch, 1977, p. xvii).

The theoretical challenge to the 'separate spheres' view arises from the implied functionalism which effectively cannot be avoided if one sees that separation as a direct consequence of industrialisation. The implication is that the separation occurred because industrialisation somehow required it, and therefore that it is functional for 'society' to keep the family as a separate, privatised sphere, whose main link with the productive world is through the male breadwinner (Safilios-Rothschild, 1976). The arguments against this classic functionalist view have been well rehearsed (Morgan, 1975, ch. 1), and it is a view no more convincing when it comes in a Marxist version, even with feminist overtones. This, to put it at its crudest, is the argument that the nuclear family with one male wage labourer and one female domestic worker is necessary to serve the needs of capital. Women's unpaid domestic labour is thus exploited by keeping them in the home, to service men and to reproduce the next generation of wage labourers. As Barrett has cogently argued, the problems with this kind of account are of functionalism and of reductionism. Women's oppression cannot be simply explained as functional for capital, because in so doing 'gender relations are reduced to an effect of the operation of capital' and thus 'phenomena of an ideological kind are reduced to their supposed economic determinants' (Barrett, 1980, p. 24). The criticism that the ideological dimension is ignored would apply equally to functionalist explanations of a non-Marxist kind. These often, whether intentionally or not, have the effect of justifying rather than analysing the *status quo*. As Leonard Barker has put it, 'Sociologists have generally accepted the phenomenal view and commonsense functionalist explanations of the family and of the society they were supposed to be analysing. They have . . . often staunchly defended the separation of the home from the rude, commercial world, stressing domestic affection and consensus' (Barker, 1977, p. 240).

The argument, that the supposed separation of the productive and domestic spheres serves to obscure other issues, can be illustrated in a number of ways. On the one hand, it directs attention towards analysing the position of women in certain ways, but away from other modes of analysis. As Edholm, Harris and Young have put it, 'the concepts we employ to think about women are part of a whole ideological apparatus which in the past has discouraged us from analysing women's work, women's spheres, as an integrated part of social production' (Edholm, Harris and Young, 1977, p. 127). But it is not only the analysis of *women's* position which is obscured by the concept of separate spheres. As Stacey (1981) has argued in her important paper on reconceptualising the division of labour, the analytical separation of the private domain of women and the public domain of men (with no way of reconciling accounts of the two) serves 'not only to hide women from sociology, but to leave sociologists of the eighties with inadeuqate conceptual, theoretical and methodological tools to analyse or explain the shifts in activities between the domestic and the public arenas' (Stacey, 1981, p. 173). There is a sense, then, in which the belief that the productive (male) sphere is separate and distinct from the domestic (female) sphere, itself is an ideologically constructed view, which sociologists reinforce whenever they take it for granted.

What are the particular implications of these debates for the analysis of wives' incorporation in men's work? Clearly it is an analysis which needs to cross the boundaries (if boundaries they be) between the spheres, as Mortimer *et al.* recognise when they describe wives' contributions to men's work as 'this pattern of assistance which has traditionally mitigated the formal separation of work and family' (Mortimer, Hall and Hill, 1978, p. 289). Rather than simply arguing that it 'mitigates' the separation of the spheres, it makes more sense to argue that this is another instance, like Davidoff's landladies, which challenges the whole basis of the assumed separation by providing instances which do not fit the analysis. Viewing it as a challenge rather than a modification clears the ground for looking at the empirical material with two particular questions in mind, to which the discussion returns later. These are: How far would it be true to argue that wives are actually part of the process of social and economic production through their incorporation in their husband's work? How far is their participation obscured by the ideological construction of work and home as two separate spheres?

In summary, the view that the productive sphere of men is quite separate from the domestic sphere of women would imply that wives *as wives* are peripheral to economic production, although they do service male wage labourers. Capital may be interested in wives as potential wage labourers themselves, especially if this means that they can be kept as a reserve army of labour, to be drawn in and out of the labour force as needs dictate (Beechey, 1977, 1978), but as wives they are consigned to the apparently non-productive domestic sphere. Examining wives' incorporation in men's work challenges that view by suggesting, to anticipate the argument somewhat, that the relationship of wives *per se* to production is actually much more central, because they are routinely incorporated in the productive process via their husbands' work.

Moving on this terrain, one is clearly coming close to a central issue which has engaged feminist theorists of women's oppression, namely, how far that oppression can be attributed solely to capitalism, or whether one introduces a whole different conceptual basis, in recognition that women's oppression is not confined to capitalist societies – namely, the concept of patriarchy in its various forms (Beechey, 1979). This study does not seek to address and evaluate those debates directly, although clearly the material discussed is relevant to aspects of them. Rather, it is hoped that it will make some contribution to the analysis of women's oppression by documenting the variety of *forms* which that oppression can take, especially in relation to male work. In that way, it is a contribution to the task identified by Barrett when she argues (in relation to cross-cultural analysis), 'What we need to analyse are precisely the mechanisms by which women's oppression is secured in different contexts, since only then can we confront the problem of how to change it' (Barrett, 1980, p. 250).

Conceptualising Wives' Incorporation: Papanek and Delphy

Moving to literature which is more specifically related to wives' incorporation, two writers in particular have been important in directly informing the analysis presented in this study.

Hannah Papanek's (1973) article represents the only real attempt in existing sociological literature specifically to conceptualise the relationship of a wife to her husband's work. This she does by developing the concept of the 'two-person career'. Her particular interest is in 'some of the aspects of American women's "vicarious achievement" through their husbands' jobs in a special combination of roles which I call the "two-person single career"' (ibid., p. 852). Papanek's main focus of interest is the participation of a wife in her husband's career both in very concrete ways, and also by becoming identified with it: she quite literally becomes part of that career. The central theme which Papanek identifies in that participation is vicariousness: a wife participates in a career which is not hers, and thereby lives through her husband in the occupational world. If he is successful, she also succeeds, again vicariously. There are therefore very apparent benefits for women in the two-person career, but such benefits are mitigated by other losses. There is, Papanek argues, 'structured ambivalence' towards a wife's participation in her husband's career on the part of all three parties involved – herself, her husband and his employer. On the one hand, wives are subject to various expectations about supporting their husbands, acting suitably in various settings, and so on, but their activities are defined as essentially outside the real world of work. Thus women's participation is simultaneously required and devalued, and consequently 'this ambivalence is particularly destructive to the self-esteem of many participants' (ibid., p. 860). The long-term consequences also entail material losses. Papanek regards the two-person career as contributing to the maintenance of women's own unequal access to occupational opportunities, despite the fact that they formally have equal access to education, because it has the effect of 'de-railing' a wife from pursuing her own career and diverts her energies into her husband's (ibid., p. 852). As a result, wives relate to the public domain of work through a peculiar relationship – they are 'gainfully unemployed': 'she is "gainfully unemployed" – that is, not considered "employed" in the economists' or census-takers' sense but nevertheless "gainfully" occupied in the context of a two-person career' (ibid., p. 863).

Papanek has made a very significant contribution in opening up this whole area and has provided some useful conceptual tools with which to think about the processes of wives' incorporation. The analysis which she offers rightly emphasises that it is concerned with 'transactions which occur at the boundary between public and private spheres' (ibid., p. 855). Moreover, she is very clear that participation in the two-person career is not a matter of 'choice, accident or conflict' but is structurally generated: 'a structural part of the middle-class wife's role' (ibid., p. 857). It is also quite consistent with prevailing cultural definitions of women's roles in marriage: 'The "two-person career" pattern is fully congruent with the stereotype of the wife as supporter, comforter, back-stage manager, home maintainer and main rearer of children' (ibid., p. 853). She directs our attention therefore to the interplay between the public and the private, and between the structural and the cultural, in developing the analysis of wives' incorporation in men's work.

The main problem with Papanek's analysis, and the main point at which mine diverges from hers, is on the issue of whether this is a middle class phenomenon. Papanek is actually not too clear on this point. Early in the paper, she argues that the two-person career is characteristic of, but not confined to, the American middle classes. But all her examples are in fact taken from this group; and more importantly, her analysis rests significantly upon seeing the two-person career in relation to the structural and cultural location of the middle classes. Indeed, the very choice of the concept of a vicarious *career* to describe the phenomenon indicates that she is in fact thinking of the middle classes. Although the concept of career is used in different ways in sociological literature, and indeed I find it a useful one to come back to later in the analysis (pp. 157–64 below), Papanek's usage of it ties her analysis not simply to the American middle classes, but particularly to that section where men climb a recognisable career ladder, in professional or bureaucratic settings. For that group, she provides a most insightful account of wives' incorporation, and one which suggests wider lines of inquiry. But the question with which her article leaves us is this: is wives' vicarious incorporation actually *confined* to professional and bureaucratic careers (in the United States or elsewhere), or has she simply provided an analysis of *one form* of incorporation?

The same question arises from the other major piece of writing which has been important in informing my own thinking: Christine Delphy's article on the main enemy (1977), and the debate which has followed it (Barrett and McIntosh, 1979; Delphy, 1980). Delphy begins from a quite different theoretical stance, and her focus is not solely upon wives' incorporation. She argues that to date (that is, in 1970, when this article was first published in France) feminists had failed to develop a satisfactory theory of women's oppression, because they had simply taken over Marxist concepts formulated outside the movement. In particular 'the specific relations of women to production have been ignored, i.e. there has been no class analysis' (Delphy, 1977, p. 1). Thus she defines her own task as 'to try to provide what the movement crucially needs at this moment: the basis for a materialist analysis of women's oppression' (ibid., p. 2). In the course of her analysis of the relations of production into which women enter, Delphy concentrates primarily upon the context of the family, and thus exposes herself to the criticism that she 'offers no distinction between the situation of wives and that of women in general' (Barrett and McIntosh, 1979, p. 102). From the point of view of wives' incorporation, however, this makes Delphy's argument particularly pertinent, especially since she gives a central place to the issue of wives' contribution to production when the unit of production is the family. She takes as her major example the traditional family farm in France, and argues that in this instance, a wife's unpaid labour is 'absolutely indispensable' to the economy of the farm, not only in her production of domestic services, but also in her participation in production for the market (Delphy, 1977, p. 5). Thus a husband appropriates his wife's labour and exchanges it in the market: 'since the production of the wife is exchanged by the husband as his own . . . her work belongs to him' (ibid., p. 7). More recent corroborative evidence of the indispensability of wives' labour to French family businesses is to be found in a study of bakers, where wives work in the shop. In the author's view, 'a baker simply cannot be a baker without a wife to act as cashier. He has to get somebody behind the counter and it has to be his wife. A wife is a woman you can trust, and one you do not have to pay . . . if the wife dies, or leaves her husband, the baker has to close the shop immediately (to find another wife takes time)' (Bertaux and Bertaux-Wiame, 1981, p. 163).

So Delphy provides an important theoretical account of the relations of production under which a wife works, in this particular instance where the family is also a unit of production. Its importance for the analysis of wives' incorporation in men's work is that it suggests a theoretical starting-point for analysing the processes whereby wives' labour is incorporated into work which is essentially their husbands'.

The problem, however, like the problem with Papanek's work, is: to how narrow a range of domestic and productive circumstances does this analysis apply? Delphy herself argues that it is a form characteristic of families which are also productive units but, since their number is decreasing, appropriation of women's labour is now mostly confined to their domestic servicing: 'nowadays, the appropriation of women's labour power is becoming limited to the exploitation (their unpaid provision) of domestic work and child rearing . . . the number of independent workers who can exchange the labour of their wives is diminishing, while the number of wage earners who cannot exchange this labour is increasing' (ibid., p. 11). Delphy more recently has further clarified her position. In answer to the charge that she builds a whole theoretical edifice upon an analysis of minority patterns, she argues that, first, her examples of family farms and family businesses primarily are counter-instances to the argument that domestic labour does not produce exchange values, and secondly, they are examples which demonstrate that wives do productive work which *can* be exchanged if their husbands require it. 'I use the example of the work of farmers' wives, which although producing goods for the market is still unpaid, to prove the falsity of the theory . . . which says that it is because domestic labour produces only "use values" and not "exchange values" that housework is not paid. I seek to stress that wives do productive work for their husbands within the labour relationship of marriage. The tasks they do vary with their husbands' needs and desires' (Delphy, 1980, p. 92). So, although Delphy defends her analysis as applicable in general to the marriage relationship, she still apparently sees the possibility of exchanging a wife's labour in the market as confined to minority instances. In particular, to return to her earlier formulation, she holds that wage labourers cannot exchange their wives' labour. This is the point at which my own analysis departs from hers. To anticipate somewhat, I think that there is a real sense in which wage labourers can and do exchange their wives' unpaid labour as their own and derive significant benefits thereby (see below, Chapter 10). For the moment, however, the main point is that this issue should remain open until the empirical evidence has been reviewed. The important questions are: How far do the relations of production under which men work make it possible or impossible for them to exchange their wives' labour? Or do men's relations of production simply alter the character and form of that exchange?

The work of both Papanek and Delphy, although in many ways addressing very different issues, raises similar questions about wives' incorporation in men's work, centring around the basis of that incorporation in the relations of production and in the marriage relationship, the different forms which that incorporation may take and the way in which those forms vary with the particular jobs that men do.

Other Sources

Whilst Papanek and Delphy are especially important in raising issues which have formed major themes of this study, other writers have suggested issues which have been of importance to particular parts of the analysis. Four of these will be mentioned more briefly.

Fowlkes's (1980) work on the wives of doctors and academics, as well as providing useful empirical evidence, suggests a threefold conceptualisation of wives' relationship to their husbands' work: the career adjunct, lending support and doing double duty. Being a career adjunct is, in her terms, the most direct form of contribution, entailing actually helping with the work, and enhancing one's husband's reputation (ibid., pp. 44–5). 'Lending support' includes a whole range of activities which 'simultaneously sustain, nurture and bolster her husband's career commitment' (ibid., p. 79). Doing 'double duty' refers to the domestic work through which a wife frees her husband to concentrate on his career (ibid., p. 124).

These are useful descriptive categories, and are reflected in the analysis developed later in this study, but there are two aspects of Fowlkes's work which make its contribution to the analysis of wives' incorporation rather limited. First, like Papanek, she assumes that contributions of wives are confined to professional careers. Secondly, she does not consider how her analysis of wives' contributions relates to the analysis of marriage *per se*. Consequently, we have no way of knowing how distinctive is the experience of being a doctor's or an academic's wife.

In more general terms, the Rapoports (1969) in an early paper have suggested a conceptual categorisation for documenting the range of possible forms which the work–family relationship can take. In particular, they offer a dichotomy between 'isomorphism' (that is, 'a similarity of behaviour patterning . . . between major life spheres') and 'heteromorphism', in which opposing or at least complementary patterns are pursued (ibid., p. 391). The issue therefore is: do family relationships take on a similar or a complementary character to the breadwinner's work relationships, and how does that vary with different jobs? This approach is very reminiscent of that taken by some sociologists of leisure, who argue that the characteristics of work itself will tend to produce a pattern of leisure time which is an extension of, an opposition to, or is neutral in respect of, that work (Parker, 1973, pp. 75–7).

In its crudest form, this argument could be open to the charge of technicism, that is, arguing that forms of technology, and work organisations associated with them, directly determine the form and character of family relationships. Young and Willmott (1973) have been accused of doing this in their rather similar account of the development of the symmetrical family (Frankenberg, 1976, p. 28). Nevertheless, the Rapoports' approach does open up a series of useful and linked questions: In what sense do features of work reach into family relationships? Is it different for men and women? Does it vary with different occupations, and if so how? What are the processes which underlie that relationship? These questions are obviously pertinent to the analysis of how men's work structures their wives' lives.

Callan's (1975) article on diplomats' wives, as well as providing an insightful empirical account, suggests an interesting concept which merits further exploration: the premiss of dedication. Callan argues that the situation of diplomats' wives is characterised by a series of paradoxes, most importantly 'the presumption that she is committed to an instituion from whose central operations she is excluded' (ibid., p. 98). This is very similar to Papanek's argument that the two-person career simultaneously requires a wife's participation and devalues it. Callan, however, argues that these paradoxes are 'to some extent resolved, or at least fudged, through a psych-social transformation of the presumption into what I call the "premiss of dedication"' (ibid., p. 98). This transformation is achieved by constituting the work which a wife is expected to do for the embassy as the outworking of naturally feminine activities, the kind of thing that any woman can do competently. Thus 'wives' dedication to diplomatic aims and activities is taken for granted in the logic of the system and then again in wives' own conscious ideology . . . I would go so far as to suggest that the premiss of dedication is the logical anchor of the complex of claims and obligations linking diplomats' wives to their husbands' employers' (ibid., p. 100). The importance of Callan's work is that, in suggesting a way of conceptualising the process which elicits contributions from diplomats' wives, she directs our attention firmly towards sexual divisions in the marriage relationship, as a key to understanding why wives are available for this kind of incorporation.

A similar line of analysis is suggested by Gowler and Legge (1978) in their article on hidden and open contracts in marriage. They argue that conventional marriage – which they define as 'the husband derives his greatest satisfaction from his job/career outside the home, while the wife derives hers . . . from within the home itself' (ibid., p. 50) – entails implicit as well as explicit contractual obligations. An important part of this hidden contract is that a wife will support her husband's work, in return for which he will provide materially for the home and take some interest in it. These contracts, they argue, in some circumstances can become explicit, but mostly they remain implicit 'with the sanction on non-compliance understood rather than spelt out' (ibid., p. 51). The notion of the hidden contract is useful, not only because it directs attention to the marriage relationship, but also because it captures something of how the relationship of a wife to her husband's work often is experienced: a mixture of externality and apparent choice, of structural forms and cultural designations. It would, however, need to be developed well beyond Gowler and Legge's analysis if it were to provide a real basis for the understanding of wives' incorporation. The important questions to ask are: how do these implicit contracts get built into marriage; what sustains them; and in what circumstances, if any, can they be overturned?

The material reviewed in this section specifies, as it were, the intellectual antecedents to this study, and raises questions to be explored further in the light of empirical evidence. Other people might have approached the topic with different antecedents, and would therefore perhaps be asking different questions. I have specified my conceptual starting-points with some care in the conviction that this will better enable others to evaluate the line of analysis which I pursue. The same applies to my use of empirical sources, to which I now turn.

Main Empirical Sources

From what has already been said, it should be quite evident that there is very little sociological work which examines empirically wives' relationship to their husbands' work. Indeed, one of the purposes of this study is to draw together such few, and rather disparate, sources as do exist.

It seems worth spelling out therefore precisely what empirical material has been most used in this book, so that readers may be able to form their own judgements about the evidence upon which the analysis is based. Only those sources which are most directly relevant and have been used most extensively are mentioned here: the bibliography can be consulted for a complete list.

Published sources which have proved most useful in this study can be divided into four categories. First, the most explicitly relevant category: work which addresses the issue of wives' relationship to men's work in particular occupations. This can be further subdivided into work by sociologists; writing for a more popular audience, usually by journalists; and historical work.

Social scientists who have studied wives' relationship to men's work are few and far between. Ray and Jan Pahl's (1971) work on managers and their wives was the first such published study, and, as far as I am aware, remains the only British book which takes this topic as a major, although not its sole, focus. Fowlkes's (1980) study of the wives of American doctors and academics provides very useful direct evidence; but its major drawback is that it is based on a very small sample of forty wives of men who have achieved some career success in these two professions. The work of Maureen Cain (1973) and Sheila Mitchell (1975) taken together provides us with useful and important evidence on police wives. Mitchell's article is based on a postal survey of police wives in Scotland, whilst Cain studied police wives in two areas in England as part of her study of the police, using the methods of interview and participant observation. Callan's article on diplomats' wives provides a valuable and insightful account of a group not normally accessible to public view. Although not confined to one occupation, Mortimer, Hall and Hill (1978) have provided a comprehensive review of empirical literature on the rather narrower topic of the relationship between men's work and wives' employment prospects. Finally, my own study of clergymen's wives, as well as providing the initial impetus for writing this book, has been used extensively as empirical evidence. Where such evidence is contained in my Ph.D. thesis, that is referenced under my former name of Spedding, in which the thesis is written.

Material written for a more popular audience obviously has to be treated with caution in academic analysis, but I have found four books particularly useful, mainly because they fill important gaps in our knowledge of occupational groups, and, at the very least, suggest where further questions might usefully be addressed. Two of these books are British: Sally Festing's (1977) account of Norfolk fishing communities, and Moorhouse's (1977) book on diplomats. Each of these contains specific discussion of wives. The other two works are American, and are used because they do explicitly address the questions about wives' relationship to their husbands' work: Seidenberg's (1973) book on corporation wives, and McPherson's (1975) on politicians' marriages. Evidence from these has to be treated with especial caution, both because it is anecdotal at best and because it uses American material only.

Historical work on wives probably could form a separate study in its own right. I have confined myself in this book almost exclusively to contemporary material, and have not attempted to provide an historical account of the development of wives' incorporation in different occupations. At various points, however, it has been useful to draw upon historical material for illustrative purposes, and the major sources which I have used are: McLeod's (1976) account of the wives of six Prime Ministers; Bamfield's (1975) lively account of British army wives, mostly in the nineteenth century; and part of the collection edited by Elbert and Glastonbury (1978), especially Glastonbury's own article on the wives of creative writers.

The second category of sociological work of which fairly extensive use has been made are studies which, whilst not explicitly addressing wives' relationship to men's work, do provide accounts of certain occupations from which some evidence about wives' incorporation can be gleaned, or at least inferred. The main danger here is in the use of empirical evidence for purposes other than its authors designed it and wrote it up. I have tried to be careful about avoiding the more obvious dangers, but readers will have to judge whether my use of this evidence seems legitimate.

Banton's (1964) book on the police supplements the evidence from Cain's and Mitchell's work; and the studies by Bechhofer *et al.* (1974a, 1974b) and Scase and Goffee (1980a, 1980b) serve to complement the work on businessmen's wives in large corporations by focusing on small businesses and the self-employed. Two further studies look at different kinds of non-manual occupations: Platt's (1976) interesting work on social researchers, and, less useful from the point of view of wives, Tunstall's (1971) book on journalists. The others are important because they introduce evidence about manual occupations: Dennis, Henriques and Slaughter's (1969) classic work on miners, although obviously out of date now, provides some important insights, and Hollowell's (1968) more recent book on lorry drivers. Salaman's (1971b) comparative study of railway workers and architects is useful especially for the discussion of the former.

Three further sources of which extensive use has been made are government reports on state employees. These are the reports of the welfare inquiries into the navy (Ministry of Defence, 1974) and the army (Ministry of Defence, 1976), and those sections of the inquiry into prisons which concern the work of prison officers (*Committee of Inquiry into the United Kingdom Prison Services*, 1979). Whilst none of these is a sociological study, they do contain empirical data of a sort which would otherwise be unavailable.

Thirdly, evidence can be gleaned from sociological studies which take the family and especially marriage (rather than occupations) as their main focus, but in doing so, say enough about men's work to enable some conclusions to be drawn about their wives' relationship to it.

Married to the Job

Most of these studies are explicitly concerned with family relationships in the middle classes: Edgell's (1980) study of middle class couples; Cohen's (1977) of spiralist couples where the husband is regularly absent; that part of Young and Willmott's (1973) study which is concerned with managing directors; and Mareau's (1976) interesting account of upper middle class couples in France. In addition, a number of useful points can be drawn from studies (again most focusing on the middle classes) which take the dual career as their major theme, following the territory mapped out by the Rapoports (1971, 1976). Extensive use has been made of certain articles in the collection edited by the Rapoports (1978), especially the article by Berger, Foster and Wallston on job-seeking strategies. Of the available American material, I have made most use of Epstein's (1971a) study of couples where both are lawyers.

Fourthly, some use has been made of self-reported material, generated by and for specific occupational groups. The possibilities for using this kind of material are endless, especially if one includes biographies. I chose not to make extensive use of these (although some illustrative material has been drawn from them), partly because of the problems of using them systematically, but mainly because they relate to a time span which would be more suitable for an historical than a contemporary study. For reasons already discussed, I rejected that approach here. I have, however, made some use of more contemporary documentation. In particular, I have read the full set of the magazine of the Soldiers, Sailors and Airmen's Families Association (SAAFA) since 1957, and of the *Prison Service Journal* and the *Police Journal* since 1968. Each of these has yielded some useful material. I have also had access to some copies, but not a full set, of the magazine of the Diplomatic Service Wives' Association, but these have been used as background reading and are not quoted in the text.

Having outlined the main empirical sources used in this study, it is perhaps worth drawing out some general points about the way in which the empirical evidence is used. First, wherever possible the discussion draws on British sources, where appropriate supplemented by American material, and in one or two cases, French. Where this has been done, it is indicated in the text. The reasons for being cautious about non-British material are not because it is considered unimportant (indeed comparative studies of this topic would be most interesting), but because the general problems about using secondary sources for purposes other than they were originally designed are compounded if they also have to cross the Atlantic. In a study which locates, as this does, a discussion of one aspect of marriage within specific economic and cultural contexts, evidence from France or America cannot be treated simply as if it was British. It can, however, be used as supportive evidence if similar patterns seem to prevail, and also to raise questions about the British context.

Secondly, the implications of men's work are discussed specifically in the context of sociological, as opposed to psychological, analysis. This is not to deny the usefulness of a parallel analysis by a psychologist; and there is certainly evidence that, for example, some men's jobs seem to have adverse effects on their wives' mental health. Doctors' wives apparently can experience psychological loss if their husband is heavily committed to his work in which they cannot share, and this sometimes leads to diagnosable psychiatric illness (Evans, 1965). Also the onset of pathological grief in doctors' wives who had nursed their husbands through a terminal illness has been partly attributed to earlier suppression of their own feelings of isolation, resulting from the belief that their husbands' patients needed them more than they did (Harari, 1981). The systematic evaluation of such findings would require a different kind of study; although of course questions about, for example, the meaning of a married woman's feelings of isolation are appropriate to sociological as well as psychological analysis.

Thirdly, in reviewing the major sources of evidence, it is apparent that, even within the limited range available, there is a particular lack of studies of working class occupations, and a corresponding over-representation of middle class jobs. This is hardly surprising, since questions about wives' relationship to men's work have barely been considered relevant to manual employment, and wives' incorporation has been assumed to be (if anything) a peculiarity of professional and bureaucratic careers. So some of the arguments which follow can move little beyond speculation in their specific application to manual work done by men. However, the general points about the uniqueness of professional and bureaucratic careers can be, and are, challenged by producing counter-instances. For this reason, the availability of reasonably extensive evidence on police wives provides a very useful counter-instance to the claim that professional careers have these unique features; whilst the case of clergymen's wives provides evidence from work outside the structures of corporate capitalism.

Structure of the Book

The central purpose of this book is to explore the different forms of wives' incorporation in men's work, and to elucidate and account for the processes which underlie them. To this end, Parts One and Two review the available empirical evidence on the two halves of the two-way relationship: Part One concentrates upon the ways in which men's work structures their wives' lives; Part Two upon wives' contributions to men's work. Neither part could be said to be a comprehensive review of the whole range of possibilities, because, as will be very apparent, there simply is an insufficient range of empirical studies to attempt quantification of the different forms of incorporation and their implications for wives. So in a very real sense this book is an exercise in mapping out the territory in the hope that others will want to explore it further. I have tried to bring together what we *do* know about wives' incorporation, and to suggest a scheme of analysis which makes sense of it. Because it is not possible to be comprehensive, the approach adopted in Parts One and Two make extensive use of what I have called 'special cases'. This is not simply a way of making a virtue out of necessity, but involves concentrating, not upon what is necessarily a *common* experience for wives, but upon what forms of incorporation are *possible* and seen as legitimate. This is important, first, because it enables us to identify the limits of the possible by examining what would seem, by most standards, to be the more extreme forms of incorporation; and secondly, because it is in these instances that some of the processes underlying wives' incorporation are most clearly revealed. The instances are special therefore, not in the sense that they are qualitatively different from the experience of most women, but often because they represent that experience writ large.

Part Three of the book draws together the empirical material with some of the questions raised by it, and attempts to develop a theoretical framework for the analysis of wives' incorporation. Although retaining this specific focus, the issues raised clearly have to be seen against various larger backcloths. I have embarked upon this study in the hope that it will contribute a different facet to our understanding of several larger issues: the relationship between the productive and the domestic spheres in a capitalist economy; the significance of forms of organisation of paid work; the context and dynamics of contemporary marriage; and above all, the economic, social and personal significance of being a wife.

Part One

Hedging Her In: How Men's Work Structures their Wives' Lives

Introduction to Part One

A wife may not be on anyone's payroll, but that is no guarantee that she will remain untouched by the organisation of paid work and its rewards. The central theme of Part One concerns one half of the two-way relationship: certain features of the content and organisation of men's work typically impose structures and constraints upon their wives' lives, obliging wives to construct their own lives within the consequent limitations.

Barker has suggested that a wife 'has her standard of living determined by [her husband], however hard she works; her rhythm, pattern and place of living are dictated by his; and what is required of her as a wife will be in considerable measure determined by his occupation' (Barker, 1977, p. 241). The chapters in Part One will explore and illustrate these processes in relation to a range of occupations, looking especially at how men's work is organised on the dimensions of time and space, and at the character of the work. Although wives' paid work is not a major focus, the effects of men's work are, it will be argued, little changed if a wife herself is in paid employment. Particular issues raised are: What specific features of men's work impose structures on their wives? How are those features related to different types of work and to particular occupations? What are the processes through which such structuring takes place?

The discussion has to be set in the context of recognising that one of the most direct effects of a man's work is the level of material provision which it affords. The observation that a married woman's living standards and lifestyle are largely determined by her husband's earnings may seem like a fine example of stating the blindingly obvious. But the very appearance of this particular piece of asymmetry (in most cases, a man's living standards are not related to his wife's earning capacity in the same way) as a taken-for-granted feature of the marriage relationship indicates that it has some significance for understanding what it means to be a wife. The assumption that a married woman will be wholly or partly dependent upon her husband's earnings is embodied in, and reinforced by, a whole range of legislation and social policy in the tax and welfare fields, as Hilary Land has so effectively demonstrated (1975, 1976, 1978).

The implications of the financial dependency of wives is a major study in its own right, and is being taken up in various ways by others (for example, Hamill, 1976; Land, 1976; Groves, forthcoming). In the context of this study, it is important to note that the range of lifestyle choices open to a wife are fundamentally governed by her husband's earnings, and will continue to be so as long as financial dependency upon one's spouse continues to be a socially approved choice for women, but not for men. In addition to the absolute level of earnings, it is interesting to note that a wife's life is structured both by the *way* her husband is paid and by the *type* of remuneration he receives.

Leaving aside the whole important issue of how a man's earnings are distributed within the family (Pahl, J., 1980), the method of payment – weekly or monthly, cash or cheque, and so on – imposes a certain pattern upon the way wives can organise their own lives and especially their expenditure. A graphic illustration of this was provided in Dennis, Henriques and Slaughter's study of a mining community in the 1950s, where wives can be seen any Friday 'alone or with small children, waiting in the vicinity of the pit gates for their husbands to give them part of their wages before they descend for the afternoon shift' (Dennis, Henriques and Slaughter, 1969, p. 198). This example illustrates not only that their husbands' earnings are crucial for these women's financial support, but also that the method of payment (the weekly wage packet, given to the employee in cash) and the common system of household allocation of resources (the allowance system, not pooling or handing over the whole wage packet) make it vital for wives to organise their lives so that they can be at the pit-head on Friday afternoons, to ensure that they receive a share of the money at the time they need it.

Such methods of payment and allocation may have a rather quaint flavour when read several decades after the research study, but there is no reason to suppose that more sophisticated methods of paying wages guarantee either that wives have access to a greater share of the male wage, or that the process of actually getting hold of their share is simplified. As Jan Pahl has pointed out (1980, p. 334), what are the implications for paying either salaries or state benefits into a bank account rather than in cash, when a wife may not necessarily have a cheque book? The significance of a wife's having direct access to some of her husband's earnings was illustrated when wives of naval ratings protested at the navy's intention to cease the historic practice of 'allotment', whereby a proportion of men's weekly earnings is paid to their wives. The Ministry of Defence view was that this practice is 'old-fashioned and unnecessary in the modern banking and computer age'. The wives, however, claimed that they sometimes have to rely completely on this direct allowance (*Guardian*, 4 August 1981).

Similarly, the type and range of remuneration which a man receives has significant implications for his wife. The size of the weekly wage packet or the monthly cheque is not the sole, or even the main, way in which a man's remuneration affects the prospects for his family's lifestyle. In the longer term, for example, prospects for home ownership are likely to be significantly related to the status and security of a man's employment. Similarly, so-called fringe benefits related to sickness benefits and pensions affect a wife's long-term financial security just as much as her husband's, especially since the right to an occupational pension as a wife or as a widow significantly alters the prospects for a woman's standard of living in her old age (Groves, forthcoming).

So, for most married women the level of material provision which accrues via one's husband's employment significantly determines the limits of possible lifestyles, both in the short and in the long term. However, the determining effect is not a simple one: the living standards of some couples must be significantly increased by the wife's own earnings, by a legacy, or by payments and gifts from other kin. Leonard has shown that the events of courtship and early married life can create a significant difference in living standards at this stage between couples where the man's job is roughly equivalent: those who have saved money for quite a long time before the wedding, who have the full backing of the bride's parents and who do not produce a child too quickly, typically being the ones whose living standards are significantly improved (Leonard, 1980, p. 250).

However, since it is still the case that comparatively few married women have an uninterrupted employment record (Dunnell, 1979, Tables, 6.4 and 6.5), and that when they do work their earnings are usually much smaller than men's (Department of Employment, 1980, Table 45), it remains the case that over the lifetime of a marriage a woman's living standards most significantly derive from the status and conditions of her husband's employment, and from the level of his earnings.

2
Time Elements: Patterns, Structures and Competition

Patterning

The structuring effect of a man's work is most clearly visible in the patterns imposed by his working hours. Of course these patterns will be modified by a number of other elements: a wife's own paid employment, having children at school, taking care of an elderly parent, and so on. Each of these in a sense sets its own timetable, and indeed family life can be seen as a series of overlapping and interacting timetables (Roth, 1963, pp. 112–14), with which wives in particular have to juggle. But the argument here is that a husband's working hours intrude in a special kind of way: in particular, the effects of a husband's working and a wife's working are not symmetrical. In so far as the couple maintain a sexual division of labour, even in a modified form, a wife normally is assigned to 'covering' domestic tasks, especially child care. This leaves her free to pursue other activities, at best, only when he is *not* at work, unless she is able to make alternative arrangements for discharging these responsibilities.

The need to 'cover' child care is not the only way in which a man's work imposes patterns on his wife's life. The man himself has to be serviced, and since many wives remain the household *managers*, even where couples share a number of specific domestic tasks, the organisation of household routines is likely to be significantly oriented to the man's working day. The traditional organisation of life in a mining community was such that 'The rhythm of domestic life is the rhythm of the working-day, of the working-week and the weekly wage packet' (Dennis, Henriques and Slaughter, 1969, p. 184). A very similar note is struck in a rather more recent account of village life in the Fens, where women's lives are organised around the needs of their husband: 'their man, and his needs, must take precedence over all else. Many men come home to lunch and expect a hot meal waiting for them' (Chamberlain, 1975, p. 71). These experiences are not confined to rural life. Deem's much more recent study of women's leisure in Milton Keynes documents the same phenomenon: 'Where men worked unsocial hours, or irregular hours, the routines of their households had to be adjusted to suit these, sometimes precluding [their wife's participation in] regular activities outside the house at particular times each week . . . or allowing only irregular attendance and also making advance arrangements to go out very difficult' (Deem, 1981, p. 7). Similarly, Hunt, in her recent study of an industrial village in the Midlands, notes that, especially where wives are not employed outside the home, 'All women in this group make some adjustments to their husband's work. The preparation and serving of meals is planned to correspond with the wage-earner's hours of work, and leisure is also tailored to fit in with his movements' (Hunt, 1980, p. 49).

The most extreme examples of 'patterning' are found where work is also based in the home (see below, chapter 4 for further discussion). In a study of British Rail resident railway crossing workers, one wife of a respondent described how her husband's working routine impinged on her day:

Mr. Johnson is able to get an average of only five hours sleep a night and Mrs. Johnson has to wake at the same time each morning to make sure he gets up . . . throughout the day Mr. Johnson is unable to move out of earshot of the block bell which warns of a train coming and is a sign to open the gates. The longest period of time that elapses without a train passing through is fifty minutes between 7.40 p.m. and 8.30 p.m. and it is during this time that Mr. Johnson eats his evening meal.

Hardly surprisingly the wife commented, 'we are both working for them [BR]' (Owen, 1980, p. 18).

Patterns and timetables imposed by a man's work obviously vary with men's working hours. Some inevitably run counter to what are otherwise considered to be 'normal' daily routines. This may be one reason why only about half of the couples interviewed in a study of shift working were happy with the husband's working shifts (Marsh, 1979, p. 83).

A particular implication of all this for a wife concerns the prospects for her own employment. In so far as she is left 'covering' in the home, and especially if child care is involved, effectively she can only take employment when he is known to be available to substitute for her: hence presumably the comparative popularity of twilight shifts (Marsh, 1979, ch. 2). The wider implications of wives having to 'fit' their lives around their husband's are discussed below (pp. 137–40); for the moment, it is sufficient to note that it happens, and that women's employment prospects are closely circumscribed by the domestic responsibilities which are assigned to them as a consequence. As Hunt puts it, in relation to wives in her study, 'One reason why women face such a lack of occupational choice is that they take on jobs to fit in with their domestic duties . . . sometimes the clash between the domestic and the paid job finds expression in people turning down promotion' (Hunt, 1980, pp. 124, 126). The extent to which a wife is *able* to fit her employment around the patterning imposed by her husband's work and the assigning of the 'covering' domestic responsibilities to her, depends somewhat upon her husband's actual working hours, especially if she can only work when she can rely on his being at home. The logistics of this must become well nigh impossible for some people: where can you find a job, for example, which fits in with a pattern of your husband's shift working, where the shifts change on a four-weekly cycle (Young and Willmott, 1973, pp. 185–6)? A closer examination of the logistics of this follows at the end of Part One (pp. 68–70), where it is related to the spatial as well as the time elements of the structures imposed by a husband's work.

Competition for the Breadwinner's Time

A 'special case' of the patterning effects of a husband's working hours is provided by jobs where there are no set working hours, or where work can 'spill over' into non-work time. In the literature on these kind of occupations there is often discussion of tensions between work and family, which in some circumstances seem to develop into direct competition over the worker's time.

A sense of this can be found in some of the work on executives, such as the Pahls' study, where they quote one of their manager's wives as saying:

> His work is not only his hobby but his life, and he has no spare time . . . he will never alter . . . In the past this has caused considerable upheavals.   (Pahl and Pahl, 1971, p. 256)

Cain notes that one general dissatisfaction with police work is that it gives 'insufficient time for family life' (Cain, 1973, p. 7), and that police wives often 'felt cheated of the companionship which they as married women were entitled to, and on behalf of their children, who were similarly entitled to a father like the others' (ibid., p. 137). The Rapoports, in discussing the family life of politicians, give an example where the balance of the pressures is in the opposite direction: an individual may be regarded as unsuitable for high office precisely because of his commitments to his wife: 'the public image of professional work tends to assume that family requirements are inherently incompatible with those of work . . . When the former British cabinet minister, Maudling, was being considered in 1963 as a possible successor to Macmillan, it was said that he was too happily married to make a good Prime Minister' (Rapoport and Rapoport, 1969, p. 390).

The conditions are set for this tension to develop into competition over the male worker's time, when his work begins to encroach significantly upon time which a wife had assumed was going to be 'free time': to be spent with the family, or to free her from total responsibility for domestic commitments. Then wives may begin to look with envy at other wives whose husbands are freer. As one of Cain's respondents put it:

> I've only one quarrel with the police force, the hours he has to work. They're just not considerate. I can't remember when he last had a rest day . . . I don't mind that so much, except when I see all these other men doing their gardens, and doing their wives windows and leaning over the fence and talking and not knowing what to do with their off duty. They should never have put our house with theirs. It's just not the same job. They do eight hours and then they're finished but my husband's never finished . . . They should put the C.I.D. houses separately. (Cain, unpublished data)

There are all sorts of reasons for a male worker to allow encroachment upon 'free' time to take place: financial gain, personal advancement, the inherent interest of the work and the attractions of the workplace. Whyte, in his well-known study of American company executives, argues that a man's living standards are much higher at work than they are at home:

> the corporation now provides a man with a higher standard of living at work than in his home – and, it might be added, a higher one than his wife enjoys. From 9 to 5 he may be a minor satrap, guiding the destinies of thousands, waited on by secretaries and subordinates; back in his servantless home, he washes the dishes. Nor is it merely the fact of his satrapy; the corporation virtually rigs it so that he can have more fun away from home. (Whyte, 1971, pp. 84–5)

The possibilities for this competition exist in a number of occupations, but its particular character and its outcome may vary.

Married to the Job

The character of the work done is probably of especial significance, since work which a wife herself values highly, or is culturally designated as especially important work, is likely to be accorded the priority in every possible case of competition with family demands. This point is made rather graphically in a book by a journalist about American politician's marriages:

> The wife of a politician can appear not only petty, but downright unpatriotic if she complains about a husband who is under the lofty illusion that he is saving the country. It is more like the dilemma faced by wives of men who immerse themselves in such professions as the ministry, science or medicine; it is tough to ask for equal time with noble endeavours as your competition.
>
> (McPherson, 1975, p. 24)

So wives of men who undertake noble endeavours (or perhaps more accurately, men with wives who *believe* that they are engaged in noble endeavours) may find that the potential competition between work and family, far from being expressed in conflict between husband and wife, results in the husband being given *more* space to get on with the great work. A wife who sees work taking over her husband's whole life, and who endorses the legitimacy of its claims upon him, may well respond by taking on *all* responsibility for domestic tasks, leaving him free to concentrate on his work. This certainly seems to be the case for clergy couples. Although one might imagine that home-based work, with no set working times, would result in a husband's taking on *more* responsibility for domestic work and child care, the opposite seems to be the case. The sentiment expressed by this wife in my study was a very common one:

> My husband would hate it if he had to fend for himself. It's not that he's not practical, he *is*; but he would not be happy having to do it, because he would be feeling all the time that he wanted to do other things. (Spedding, 1975, p. 295)

In this study, it was very clear that the potential competition between work and family became expressed very much in a presumed dichotomy between spending time on church work and spending time on household work or child care. Since a clergyman's work is based in the home, and work can be done at any time of day or even night, the situation is structured so that any performance of domestic tasks appears to be an *alternative* to work; and a clergyman's wife who suggests that her husband might take on some of these tasks feels that she is taking him away from his work. Since most clergymen's wives value their husband's work highly, it is hardly surprising that their response is to create the domestic conditions which ensure that he is not distracted (Spedding, 1975, ch. 12). They provide a good illustration of how the combination of flexible working hours and home-based work (see below, pp. 53–7 for fuller discussion) can create a *more* rigid sexual division of labour, not less, despite Young and Wilmott's utopian belief that these are precisely the conditions which will create greater symmetry in family life and especially in the division of labour between husband and wife (Young and Willmott, 1973, p. 272).

A further twist to the potential competition for the male breadwinner's time is provided where his work has the particular characteristic that he is always, or considers himself to be, potentially 'on duty', even when he is officially 'off'. This is an important characteristic of certain occupations, especially where the worker has a particular skill which may be needed at any time, perhaps in emergencies. However, people engaged in other types of work may also regard themselves as potentially always on duty, especially if they hold some position of responsibility where they would always want to be on the spot to take a particular *decision*, even if no specialised skill is involved. An example of this can be found in Young and Willmott's study, where a computer manager, whilst officially on duty at certain times only, clearly considered himself responsible for his computer at all times:

> My hours are supposed to be from nine to five past five. I arrive every day between eight and eight thirty, and I never leave before six thirty, or seven in the evening. I come in here one Saturday morning out of two, and sometimes both. Occasionally I look in on a Sunday to see if everything is going as it should be. Last Saturday I worked from nine thirty until one. Go on – tell me I'm a fool. My wife does.   (Young and Willmott, 1973, p. 136)

For people with those kinds of responsibilities, the telephone provides what Young and Willmott have called a 'means of trespass' between work and home (ibid., p. 167), since it affords the opportunity to call them into work. A graphic illustration is provided by one of Fowlkes's respondents, an American doctor's wife:

> It's pretty bad when you get in bed and you're making love and you hear the g- d- phone ring. It interrupts arguments, it interrupts meals, but sex is the ultimate of interruptions.
>   (Fowlkes, 1980, p. 84)

The opportunities for trespass by telephone are not limited to men in professional occupations. One of Cain's respondents described how her policeman husband could be called out by his superiors:

> One morning I really had a row with them about it. He was off duty but had been called out early from something or other, and do you know, at half past six that phone started ringing and I said, no, I'm not going to answer it, and that went on until half past eight. But I wasn't going to answer it; that was his rest day. Anyway, at half past eight I did answer, and that was the inspector, . . . And he was really rude to me. "Didn't you hear the phone ringing?" he said. "Yes" I said, "Why didn't you answer it then" he said. Just like that. "I was busy", I said, "with the children". "Where's your husband then", he said, really rude to me you know. "He's out", I said, "anyway, he's on rest day". "Where's he gone?". "If you must know, to help an old lady with moving", I said. I never did tell him where he'd gone. Why should I? He was off duty.   (Cain, unpublished data)

The ethos of being always available opens up the opportunity for work to trespass, and this is a characteristic feature of a number of occupations. Haberstein's study of American funeral directors provides a good example here, and no doubt the same would be true in Britain:

> Clients, particularly of 'local funeral homes', want the services of a funeral director who they know personally, or who has served their families in the past. Consequently, such a funeral director feels the need to be constantly at hand: there is really no moment of his life safe from the demands of his clientele.
>
> (Haberstein, 1962, pp. 241–2)

The clergy are another example of an occupational group where constant availability is considered essential. Their situation provides an illustration of how the competition for the breadwinner's time can become focused around one particular issue: arranging time off. The unreliability of time off was an issue discussed with some enthusiasm by many of the clergy wives in my study. In the sample of wives of non-conformist ministers, twenty-four out of thirty-three wives said that the husband took *no* regular time off, and only three took as much as one day a week. The issue was a major cause for complaint and concern among all clergy wives, both anglican and nonconformist, and it was often blamed upon a husband's lack of personal organisation and discipline. However, for clergy the situation is compounded by adherence to the ethic of the availability of the minister at all times; one respondent put it like this:

> Theoretically Monday is the day he would like to set apart, but more often than not, it's hopeless. I suppose we don't discipline ourselves enough on this and say, right, we're having this day off whatever happens, it can't work like that. Last December we were all set to go Christmas shopping, and someone unexpectedly died. And of course by the time we had visited the widow, and one or two other people . . . But what can you do in those circumstances? You can't say, I'm sorry, it's my day off. (Spedding, 1975, p. 302)

The competitive elements set up in situations where the worker has to be constantly available serve as perhaps the most extreme example of a point which has become apparent through this consideration of the patterning effects of a man's working hours: the structures imposed by the time dimension are overlaid both by the character of the particular occupation, and the spatial relationship between home and work. The next chapter involves a more specific consideration of the implications of the character of the work.

3

Work Characteristics: Implications Inside and Outside the Home

Work Characteristics and Domestic Life

An examination of the literature on occupations suggests three common ways in which the characteristics of work can 'spill over' into non-work life. These are: being mentally 'at work' for most of the time; the replication of patterns of working relationships; escaping *from* work and the need to counteract its effects.

The potential effects of bringing home the *consequences* of work, if not the work itself, are widely recognised in our culture, and the ability of some individuals to 'leave their work behind' at the factory gates or the office door is often much admired. Far more people can bring home work in their heads than bring it in their briefcases, and the possibility that a worker can be mentally 'at work' when overtly engaged in non-work activities presumably occurs in almost any occupation, since he or she may be thinking about features of the work itself, or about aspects of the relationships located in the workplace. A woman also may 'bring home' her work in this way, but it will be argued that its effects upon others in the household are unlikely to be the same as the effects of her husband's work, because of the continued significance of his being cherished as the family breadwinner.

Although one might find examples of carrying over the effects of working *relationships* in almost any occupation, examples of being mentally 'at work' are found mainly in literature about occupations seen as inherently stressful, or where the worker carries quite a high degree of individual responsibility. Morris, writing of the experience of prison officers, sees this as partly a two-way traffic of problems, the tensions of which can best be absorbed by wives, not the men themselves:

Work problems spill over into his leisure time and private problems may be accentuated by his work experience and spill over into working hours, thus placing a great strain on marriages. It is constantly asserted by officers with long service that *an understanding and tolerant wife is the best asset a man can have in this job.*

(Morris, 1963, p. 8) (my italics)

Sometimes, if work is regarded as an intrinsically enjoyable experience, the ability to be 'at work' when apparently doing something else may be welcomed by the worker. Examples of this were given by some of Young and Willmott's managing directors:

When I'm in the bath or mowing the lawn, I'm often trying to figure out some problem or other.

If you saw me very happily sitting in the garden with a drink at my side I might be thinking over a problem. If you came along beside me you might be talking to me for ten minutes and I wouldn't hear you, I'd be so concentrated.

(Young and Willmott, 1973, p. 166)

Enjoyable and welcome as this facility may be for the worker, it may not be so for others in the household. Another respondent in the same study recognises that the effects may be unpleasant for his wife, but seems to regard this as part of some sort of normal domestic pattern:

One has problems. You might think about them and drift off into a haze and don't pay any attention to what your wife is telling you. I said I never take work home – that's true, not paperwork. But unfortunately it remains in my head. There are *the usual domestic problems* as a result. (ibid., pp. 166–7) (my italics)

The second way in which characteristics of work carry over into non-work time is through the continuation or replication or particular patterns of relationships. A number of studies provide examples of out-of-work friendships being based on workplace relationships almost exclusively: ranging from the mobile middle classes in Bell's (1968) study to a stable working class community, especially if it is based mainly on one industry. Salaman, in his study of architects and railway workers, quotes one railwayman's wife as saying:

It's railways, railways, railways with him. All railwaymen are like it, they just want to get together and talk railways. As though they didn't have enough. If you want to find out about railways, ask the wives. We're the ones who've had railways all these years.

(Salaman, 1971b, p. 398)

This wife clearly felt that not only her husband's leisure time but also her own life was dominated by his work.

Another way in which patterns of relationships are carried over from the workplace is not through *actual* friendships, but when the *style* of relationship is replicated in non-work settings. The Rapoports suggest this in one of their earlier papers: 'Presumably there are soldiers who organise their families like platoons, computer technicians who program their families as they do their machines, and boxers who use physical violence at home' (Rapoport and Rapoport, 1969, p. 392). No doubt there are, but it is fairly difficult to find actual examples of this in the literature, and there is a real possibility of caricature by overstatements here. Banton gives an example in his study of the police, when he quotes a respondent:

I'll tell you another thing that I've noticed myself doing, if there is something wrong in the house you begin to question your wife as if you were questioning a suspect. It's actually true – you ask a police sergeant – you begin to get into a routine.

(Banton, 1964, p. 208)

An example of the replication of police relationships in the home is given by one of Cain's respondents:

Policemen make bad fathers. They can't help bringing the job into the home. They're too strict. It's alright with some children, but it's a nightmare with our son, especially when he was about twelve. We had dreadful rows. My husband's unimaginative and my son's just the opposite. My husband's very rigid. I've got a psychiatrist friend who said it was probably the thought of being a policeman going through his head.

(Cain, unpublished data)

In a rather less direct way, Fowlkes suggests that the style of professional relationships adopted by doctors results in the development of a style of family life in which they remain emotionally disengaged (Fowlkes, 1980, pp. 162–3).

The case of the clergy of the Church of England provides an example – albeit quite a rare one perhaps – where a worker is formally *expected* to replicate work relationships in the home, since he is specifically required to promise at the time of his ordination that he will try to create his home as a model for the church. In the modernised version of the ordination service, this reads, 'Will you strive to fashion your own life and that of your household according to the way of Christ?' (Church of England, 1980, Ordination of Priests, p. 358).

The examples so far have been about continuities between work and home and their implications for wives, but plenty of examples of the opposite can be found – the use of non-work time and relationship to *get away from* work. The distinction developed by the Rapoports between isomorphism and heteromorphism is relevant here (Rapoport and Rapoport, 1969, p. 391). Whilst this perhaps has some use as a conceptual tool, it would be misleading to suggest any individual or occupational group is characterised *either* by similarity between home and work *or* by contrast. It seems more likely that some features of work will be replicated and others contrasted, and the more interesting questions centre around the way in which the two are combined, although insufficient detailed empirical data exists for clear patterns to be identified.

The theme that the home is a place where workers can escape from the work and recover from its effects is a common one. The home often makes its appearance in this form in structural functionalist analyses of the family and work and, as Dorothy Smith writes, commenting on Smelser's work, 'Essentially . . . from this point of view, the home is a place where people are stored when they are not at work, where they are maintained and serviced, fed and cleaned, where they are psychologically repaired and the injuries of daily routine and the tensions generated on the job made good' (Smith, 1973, p. 10). In this account the wife of course is the key figure, since she creates the home as the kind of place where recuperation is possible. Dennis *et al.*'s account of miners' wives stresses that they feel they must create a comfortable home to contrast with the rigours of their husbands' working environment (Dennis, Henriques and Slaughter, 1969, p. 179). The same pattern can be repeated in a completely different occupation, as when the wife of an airline pilot described the effects of his work, and her response to them:

I often say BOAC is his mistress. He gets very tired. The first day home I have learned to keep quiet and not mention any problems. He still has the noise of the jet engines in his ears. His face is white and fatigued.   (Young and Willmott, 1973, p. 165)

In so far as wives do respond to these 'needs' created in work by providing what is regarded as an appropriate contrast – a comfortable, undemanding and well-organised home – they can be seen as contributing their labour towards the production of a husband with a greater capacity for work. This point will be taken up again in Part Two. The other side of it however is that, in so far as it is accepted that a legitimate (and even an important) part of being a wife is to create the kind of domestic setting which will provide for the male worker's work-generated 'needs', then a wife's life is further structured and constrained thereby.

Public Figures

Some occupations are characterised by their ability to define the worker as a 'public figure'. Although this undoubtedly is a minority experience, it is worth looking at its consequences since, it will be argued, it is an extreme example of a wife's life being structured by her identification with her husband's work.

Being a public figure essentially means being defined in terms of work for the purposes of almost all social contacts. Such situations seem to be produced by a combination of characteristics of the work itself, and the setting in which it takes place. Doctors, for example, may find it easier to establish a private identity if they work in a large hospital than if they are general practitioners, and probably find it most difficult of all if they work as a GP in a rural community. The rural doctors studied by Horobin and McIntosh certainly found this difficult. What the authors call their 'embeddedness in the community' had both its rewards and its problems, and meant that they could never really be off duty (Horobin and McIntosh, 1977, p. 96).

Banton has called this phenomenon the 'contamination' of the private person by the occupation (Banton, 1964, p. 197). In his own analysis of the police, he suggests that there are two particular characteristics of police work which require that the police be 'set apart' to some extent: they have access to privileged information, and they do a job which requires that everyone be treated on an equal footing (ibid., ch. 7). If he is correct, then a number of other occupations have the same characteristics: doctors, clergy and Members of Parliament, for example, all do jobs in which they have privileged access to information, and are assumed to treat everyone alike. The reason why these occupational features have the effect of 'setting apart' the incumbents would seem to be the presumed dangers of breach of confidentiality and of favouritism. Those dangers are greatly enhanced if the work is conducted in a settled and identifiable community, and it is in those settings especially, therefore, that certain jobs carry with them the 'public figure' status, where the individual is not available for some of the normal processes of community life, like purveying gossip or taking sides in local disputes. As Banton observes, 'The policeman, like the clergyman, is required to be a bit better than everyone else' (ibid., p. 190).

It would be misleading, however, to imply that the processes of contamination apply only to professional work, or only to stable 'community' settings. *All* doctors, for example, will be subject to the expectations of confidentiality and impartiality. But those who work in cities and in hospitals do have more opportunities to develop a lifestyle in which they can foster alternative identities. The use of the police as one of the main examples of contamination should already have underlined that this does not apply solely to professional work. Prison officers are another group to whom it can apply, and again the inability to talk freely about work provides one of the main mechanisms by which they are set apart. 'Even if the prison officer wants to have social relationships with ordinary people outside, the prison officer is under a special kind of constraint. His work has a strong, macabre kind of fascination for the ordinary citizen, yet the officer, bound by the Official Secrets Act, cannot talk freely about his job as can the busman, foreman or office worker' (Morris, 1963, p. 8). One important mechanism for the setting apart of certain non-professional workers is the wearing of a uniform, which enables them to be identified as 'public figures' and distinguished from other members of the working classes, with whom they might otherwise be confused because of their accent and manner. Thus Morris notes that prison officers are identified with the prison even on their journeys to work through the wearing of a uniform (ibid., p. 8). Some professional workers who are set apart also wear a uniform, although they may well not wear it all the time: the clergy, for example. For professional 'public figures' a uniform is less necessary, since their accent and manner (produced through their background and training) should be enough to mark them out.

If 'public figures' are contaminated by their work, it is equally true that their wives experience a kind of vicarious contamination. This means that they experience some of the consequences of being a public figure without having been appointed, elected, or paid to be one. Nevertheless, in certain circumstances a wife will be expected to behave *as if* she had been. Papenek refers to this as situations where 'the wife's participation is almost, but not quite, formally institutional-ised – the ambassador's wife, the mayor's wife, the wife of a large foundation representative abroad, the wife of a company president, the First Lady, and so on. All of these women are expected to give acknowledged public performances, as are the wives of political candidates' (Papanek, 1973, p. 862). Examples of this are discussed further in Part Two, since these are situations where, very clearly, wives make direct contributions to their husbands' work.

What effects does this vicarious contamination have upon a wife? In various situations these seem to include: expectations that she will conduct herself 'appropriately', being held at arm's length by other people, being treated with deference or hostility. In short, she seems to experience in routine social relationships the same patterns which her husband experiences in his particular occupational location. But there is an additional element for his wife, since her vicarious setting apart means she is also on show as a *wife*, and liable to be subject to additional expectations as a consequence.

Studies of police wives provide good illustrations of feeling that one is expected to act in certain ways – to be a bit better than everyone else – because one is married to policemen. 'A higher standard is expected of the policeman and his family in many matters, and they are all very much aware of this . . . the country policeman is highly vulnerable to criticism from his neighbours' (Whittaker, 1964, p. 125). In Mitchell's survey, although about a quarter of all wives felt that 'the nature of their husband's job affected the way they were treated by neighbours', Mitchell argues that the extent to which a police wife will be seen as an extension to her husband depends upon the 'visibility of the police family's status' (Mitchell, 1975, p. 84), so that wives of city police are less at risk.

Wives of the clergy also feel very much under scrutiny about their own conduct, and that of their families. They often feel particularly uncomfortable on their children's behalf. As one anglican said,

> They expect you to do what they won't do. They expect clergy kids to be marvellous and do this, that and the other; quite honestly they're just ordinary kids and I think they want an ordinary kind of life.　　　　　　　　　　　　　　　　　　　　　(Spedding, 1975, p. 304)

However, it is not easy to simply dismiss these kind of expectations since they also, by implication, put a wife under scrutiny as a good mother. As one baptist minister's wife admitted,

> I think there are times when ministers and their wives expect more of their children, or tend to want them to conform, simply because of what Mrs. So and So will say. And often people do look upon them and criticise them if they are not perfectly behaved and so on.　　　　　　　　　　　　　　　　　　　　　　　　　(loc. cit.)

Wives of the clergy actually vary very much in their response to being the wife of a public figure. In my study, they were fairly evenly divided on the suggestion that a clergyman's wife ought to make her home and family a model for the rest of the congregation or parish: the majority rejected this idea, some reacting against it strongly, but two-thirds accepted it as an ideal to which to aspire, with anglicans and baptists especially likely to hold this view (ibid., pp. 304–6).

A particular problem for wives of 'public figure' men is to find a basis upon which social relationships can be conducted, and especially to make friends. The two key elements here seem to be: the feeling that one is being kept at arm's length by other people; secondly, the recognition that it might be regarded as inappropriate to have close friends in the community where one's husband holds a 'public' position.

The clergymen's wives in my study reflected both of these very clearly; for example:

> I think that sometimes people don't talk to you about the ordinary things that you would want to talk about . . . They just think of the minister and his wife as being something different, not one of us.
>
> (ibid., p. 314)

The feeling that one is regarded as not available for normal friendly relations is paralleled by queries about the appropriateness of friendship. Although clergy wives are about equally divided about whether they ought to 'allow' themselves to have local friends, almost all recognised this as extremely problematic. The underlying reasons for this relate to the key features of 'public figure' jobs – confidentiality and impartiality. The consequent setting apart applies equally to the clergy wife – for her to have friends offers the potential for divulging confidences or showing favouritism, both of which would be as inappropriate for her as for her husband. One respondent, a woman in her twenties with three young children, described vividly the kind of dilemma in which this had placed her:

> We were taught at theological college, by the principal's wife, that it is wrong to have close friends; and for the first eighteen months here I was extremely careful. I found it very, very hard going, and I had a terrific struggle with this problem: should I or should I not? There was one girl I was particularly drawn to – we get on like a house on fire, we are just the same sort of people. I sort of warded it off for ages and ages, but I *needed* friendship locally, and she was a Christian. And in the end I just thought, well, this is ridiculous. I analysed my reasons for it, and in the end I could find absolutely no

reason for not having a close friend. Otherwise it makes you somehow different, if you decide you're going to be aloof, it adds to the picture of being different. So I gave in in the end, and it worked out really well.   (ibid., p. 318)

It is clear from this that the woman involved went through considerable personal agony as a result of the presumed bar on friendship deriving from her husband's job; and it is interesting that, even when she decided to make a friend, she thought of this as 'giving in'.

Wives of other 'public figures' also experience similar dilemmas, and the feeling of being kept at arm's length. One police wife described the feeling of 'restraint when they know that my husband is in the police' (Mitchell, 1975, p. 85), and one-quarter of Mitchell's sample felt that the nature of their husbands' job affected the way they were treated by neighbours (ibid.).

A further way in which wives experience the effects of a 'public figure' husband is by being, as it were, bracketed with him, and treated with the same kind of mixture of deference, awe, sycophancy, or hostility with which he is treated. This may be quite pleasant if it is deference, but less so if it is hostility. Despite the scepticism of the May Committee on this point, prison officers believe that other people often treat them with hostility because of their job (*Committee of Inquiry into the United Kingdom Prison Services*, 1979, para. 8.2), although the consequences for their wives are not spelled out. Police wives talk similarly about reflected hostility. In the milder examples they are simply given a wide berth, as with this example of a police wife going into a local shop:

> There'll be the usual huddle in the middle of the floor and conversation going on. It dries up when they go in, and everyone moves up to the counter to be served. After they have been able to get served, they hear the hubbub break out again after they come out. I don't know if it's hostility or sheer suspicion.
>
> (Banton, 1964, p. 200)

A somewhat more extreme example was given to Mitchell by a city police wife:

> I could not leave my house for them shouting abuse at me and if they were near enough they spat on me. When I washed my steps or the close, the children came and urinated on them – they also rubbed excreta on my doormat.   (Mitchell, 1975, p. 86)

Whilst not wishing to suggest that incidents of this sort are necessarily a common occurrence, the very fact that they *can* happen indicates the extent to which wives of men in certain occupational settings do become very closely identified with their husband's work, and experience the consequences of it vicariously.

Finally, what strategies are possible for wives who wish to mitigate, or more easily to accommodate themselves to, the effects of vicarious contamination? First, one can try to turn it to one's own advantage. Wives of men who are regarded as important figures nationally or locally presumably can use their position in a variety of ways, and some may become quite skilful at it. Wives of somewhat lesser public figures can also turn it to their advantage: some of Mitchell's police wives said that their association with the police acted as a good character reference when they were seeking employment.

> You automatically gain a position of trust and respect by employers.
> (Mitchell, 1975, p. 88)

Secondly, wives develop strategies for handling social relationships, in which they try to minimise the significance of their 'wife of' identity. The two main ways in which this seems to be done are concealment and seeking out the company of others in a similar situation. Concealment is a strategy which seems to be used in situations where it is important to preserve a distance from the work – on holiday, for example, which for some workers may be the only time when they are really 'off'. A police respondent in Banton's earlier study described the consequences of failure to conceal successfully:

> I remember being in a boarding house up in Arbroath and it was nice and sociable until someone asked my wife what I did, and as soon as the police were mentioned you could sense a change in atmosphere . . . I had to make a conscious effort to overcome what happens to you then.
> (Banton, 1964, p. 200)

Attempts to conceal are a response to recognising that one's occupational identity, or the vicarious one attributed to a wife, will be regarded as one's 'real' identity, or at least the one which takes precedence over all others (Mitchell, 1975, p. 88). Failed attempts to conceal are experienced as a kind of unmasking, as a relevation of the key piece of information about onself.

Concealment is hazardous because of the constant danger of unmasking, and once the vicarious occupational identity is revealed, a wife probably will find it very difficult to establish her own identity in any other light. So it is not surprising that wives commonly adopt the alternative strategy and seek company among what Mitchell classes 'safe categories', people among whom they have a personal identity, primarily long-standing friends and family (Mitchell, 1975, p. 88). The company of wives of men in the same occupation is also sought, since they too constitute safe categories. Morris has described how social life for many prison officers and their wives centred on the company of like others. 'One of the striking things about the staff community is that whether it is in a city prison or in an isolated country district, socially it is just as remote from the outside world. The reference groups tend to be the staff and families of other institutions, thus coachloads of officers and their wives travel between the social clubs of Pentonville, Wandsworth, Brixton and Wormwood Scrubs' (Morris, 1963, p. 8). Much more recently, the May Committee still found prison officers, including governors, to be 'a somewhat inward-looking group' (*Committee of Inquiry into the United Kingdom Prison Services*, 1979 para. 8.3), and firmly placed the blame for this upon the officers themselves: 'we think the tendency of members of the service primarily to seek out each others' company is substantially a matter of choice and convenience; it does not necessarily flow from their occupation' (ibid., para. 8.2). The committee apparently fails to recognise a crucial point: what appears to an individual as the most convenient and congenial choice is itself partly a product of the conditions under which the work takes place.

These strategies for forming friendships are very important, because they offer some pointers to the process of bargaining of identities, and the extent to which wives are constrained by features of their husbands' work when they undertake this process. Certainly it seems that being the wife of a public figure means that one's room for manoeuvre is very tightly circumscribed.

4
Spatial Elements:
Aspects of the Location
of Home and Work

The Location of Work and Home

Despite the assumption that industrialisation has effectively constituted work and home into separate 'worlds', in practice the two are
very much more separate for some people than for others. This section
concentrates on exploring how far the character of a wife's relationship
to her husband's work varies with the geographical location of that
work.

The most obvious example of closeness of work to the home is where
the husband actually uses the home as his work-base. That situation
has special kinds of implications for wives, which are discussed below
(pp. 53–9). But the removal of a husband's work from the home in
itself does not guarantee that a wife's life is not structured and
constrained by it: indeed, the character of those constraints may
simply be altered. Where the husband's work is located at a
considerable distance from the home, for example, it becomes much
more difficult to develop a lifestyle which includes shared child care,
even if both spouses want this (Gowler and Legge, 1978, p. 49). The
most extreme examples occur when work is organised so that the
worker has to be away from home for whole blocks of time – in the
fishing industry, the oil industry, or in the services, for example. These
examples point to the logistics of handling the overlapping constraints
of both the time and spatial dimensions of one's husband's work. This
is considered further in the concluding chapter of Part One (pp.
68–70), in the discussion of how wives develop coping strategies. In
this chapter, the emphasis primarily is on the spatial dimension.
Special cases are drawn from variations in the possible physical
location of home and work (home as work-base; tied accommodation;
institutional settings), and the implications of regular *re*location of
home, by following one's husband's work.

Although for the most part the emphasis here is upon the physical location of work, it must be acknowledged that this is partly mitigated by the degree of separateness between the spouses in knowledge or experience of that work. That is, how far is a wife effectively kept at arm's length from features of her husband's work? The most obvious examples of this are occupations where confidentiality is assumed to be a feature of all or part of the husband's work, and therefore a wife is explicitly excluded from knowledge of that work, if he adheres to the custom strictly.

That kind of distancing can take place whatever the physical location of the work – indeed, it can happen even if the worker sees clients at home, provided that privacy is possible within the domestic setting. It is more likely, however, that the physical location of work away from home will automatically exclude wives from knowledge of certain aspects of it, especially if work takes place in a setting which is not publicly accessible. Dennis *et al.* demonstrate that miners' wives knew little of their husbands' work, since no women were employed underground. Moreover, since few wives were themselves in paid employment, they had little knowledge of the productive relations of industry since 'productive work in Ashton . . . is with a few exceptions the exclusive realm of menfolk' (Dennis, Henriques and Slaughter, 1969, p. 184). In some situations, the distancing of women from work is reflected in cultural beliefs and practices. Clark's study of a Yorkshire fishing village shows that the occupational beliefs of the fishing community included the belief that it is unlucky just to see a woman on the way to work, and such a sighting can result in the fisherman's not putting to sea (Clark, 1982, ch. 8).

In one sense, such examples are rather extreme cases of the invisibility of work, but a husband's work may be just as effectively invisible to a wife who spends her days in suburban Surrey or Hertfordshire, while he travels to work in central London. Indeed, Gowler and Legge have argued that such circumstances may, if anything, make a man's work *more* remote from the home, since 'in a white-collar or manual job he may typically work at activities difficult to define or describe' (Gowler and Legge, 1978, p. 49). They contrast this with a docking or mining community, where the organisation for which her husband works may have considerable impact upon the area where a wife lives.

The physical separation of work and home can be bridged to some extent by a husband's *talking* about his work. How much he does so is not solely a matter of personal preference, but is related to the character of that work (for example, norms of confidentiality, the ease with which one can describe what one actually does), and also possibly to cultural prescriptions about discussing work. Komarovsky has described how American blue-collar workers commonly exclude their wives from knowledge about their work (Komarovsky, 1967, pp. 151–5), and Porter's study of wives of men in industrial dispute has underlined that there is considerable variation in wives' consciousness of their husbands' work experience. She warns that 'there was no necessary or automatic direct correspondence between the consciousness of the wives and the fact that their husbands were on strike . . . it is dangerous to generalise about the relationship of men's and women's consciousness as if it had a simple one-to-one correspondence' (Porter, 1978, p. 271). So the relationship in terms of physical location between a man's work and his home does not straightforwardly include or exclude wives. The relationship is compounded by other features which effectively keep wives, to a greater or lesser extent, at arm's length from knowledge about and experience of their husbands' work.

Special Case: the Geographically Mobile

If couples adhere to the cultural norm of locating the household near to the husband's work, then work which involves him in frequent geographical moves imposes a special kind of patterning upon his wife's life. Some authors have focused upon the implications for her own employment, especially in so-called 'dual-career' couples (Rapoport and Rapoport, 1971, 1978; Mortimer, Hall and Hill, 1978; Brezeskwinski, 1981), but clearly there are possibilities for a wife's being affected in other ways.

In a discussion firmly embedded in an American structural functionalist account of the family, Blood makes this bizarre observation on Whyte's study of mobile executives: 'the *central* adjustment for the wife is transferring her housekeeping operations from one house to another. Modern [removal] vans make this less difficult than it once was' (Blood, 1969, p. 223) (my italics). The good company wife apparently is a woman whose life is totally centred around domestic concerns, busy creating a comfortable nest suitable for transfer to any new location, where she will be equally happy since the home is her world. Possibly that may ring truer as a picture of middle class America in the 1950s than it does of Britain in the 1980s. But in looking at the implications of a husband's geographical mobility for his wife, we certainly need to go beyond the assumption that the main issues are practical considerations about how to move the furniture.

The major question posed in this chapter is: what are the implications for wives of a geographically mobile lifestyle? That question can only properly be considered, however, by looking at the contexts in which mobility takes place. In particular: What are the circumstances in which workers are geographically mobile? What choice do wives have about that mobility?

Although geographical mobility of workers obviously does have a class dimension, it should not be too readily assumed that a geographically mobile lifestyle is a unique characteristic, or the sole prerogative, of the middle classes. By no means all the middle classes move around the country at frequent intervals, as has long been recognised in sociology since Watson (1964) developed the spiralist/burgesses distinction and Bell's (1968) study confirmed its significance empirically. It is not necessary to engage here with the debates about whether a dichotomy such as spiralist/burgess is too simplistic (Pahl and Pahl, 1971, pp. 41–5), but both theoretical and empirical discussions around this topic serve to emphasise that constant geographical mobility is by no means the universal experience of the middle classes. Indeed, there are at least three different kinds of circumstances in which male workers move, only the first of which seems particularly characteristic of the middle classes: to obtain promotion (either with the same or a different employer); to seek new work; to meet the employer's requirements.

These three different reasons for moving leave the male workers with differing degrees of choice about whether to go; or perhaps more accurately, present him with different *kinds* of choices. A decision about moving to seek new work after redundancy, for example, is a very different kind of decision from one which relates to promotion: at its starkest, the former involves securing a basic livelihood, the latter simply improving an existing one. In some occupations, moves of the third type (to meet employer's requirement) leave the worker effectively with *no* choice, sometimes formally with none.

The clearest cases of 'enforced' geographical mobility can be seen in the armed forces. In a postal survey carried out in connection with a review of army welfare, the frequency of moves (referred to in military terminology as 'turbulence') was shown to be considerable: over half of all families had moved at least three times in the previous five years (Ministry of Defence, 1976, para. 132). Similarly in connection with an inquiry into navy welfare, wives of young ratings (husbands aged 18–25) reported that they had moved on average once a year since marriage, and wives of young officers (husbands aged 22–30) had moved just over once a year (Ministry of Defence, 1974, paras 137 and 140).

The frequency of moves is very striking here, and the context in which they take place gives them a particular character: the move occurs simply because the worker is deemed to be needed elsewhere. The same kind of moves can happen in the police, sometimes at short notice. Transfers of that sort sometimes are regarded as 'punishment moves' consequent on a previous incident in which the officer has gained the disapproval of his superiors (Cain, 1973, p. 153). This emphasises the degree of discretion which an employer (or in this instance a hierarchical superior) potentially can use in making decisions about geographical mobility: processes of consultation notwithstanding, the decision ultimately is completely out of the worker's own hands.

Undoubtedly for some people, geographical mobility (for whatever reason) is a way of life; as it was for one of the manager's wives in the Pahls's study who observed, 'when the curtains get dirty, I begin to think of moving' (Pahl and Pahl, 1971, p. 53). Where this happens, how far is it open to wives to take an active part in shaping their husbands' job choice, and pattern of mobility?

There is some evidence that in the case of individual decisions, couples commonly report the wife's active participation in discussions about moving, as befits adherents to the model of the companionate marriage. The managers and their wives in the Pahls's study reported that decisions about a possible move were always discussed between them before a decision was made, although the relative contribution of each partner is not always clear (Pahl and Pahl, 1971, p. 59). They also note that most couples regard the *final* decision as lying with the man: although wives say that they have the power of veto, they rarely use it (ibid., p. 61). This is hardly surprising of course, since the whole situation is one of structured inequity between the partners: the husband, as worker, has knowledge of considerations specific to the *job*, as well as to the home, and his view of the comparative advantages and disadvantages of the move will almost inevitably be more compelling than his wife's. Nevertheless, the Pahls believe that their study shows that wives are 'not simply passive participants in the moves in which their husbands' careers may involve them' (ibid., p. 67). That conclusion would be supported by studies where both partners are working, and especially where both are attempting to follow reasonably orderly careers, decisions about moving take on a special character, and may result in complex strategies designed to enable the jobs, as well as the marriage, to continue (Rapoport and Rapoport, 1971; Berger, Foster and Wallston, 1978).

So even in situations where the move seems relatively optional, the amount of choice available to a wife may be more apparent than real: still less where the move entails seeking new work, or meeting the employer's requirements. Moreover, studies of the way in which decisions are made about any *individual* move may overstate a wife's ability to shape the *overall* pattern of her husband's mobility. Being able to agree whether or not a *particular* move is desirable is not the same as having a real choice about pursuing a lifestyle of continuous geographic mobility rather than one of relative immobility, even if each individual move is apparently optional, and 'only' for promotion.

The pressures upon a wife to acquiesce to a mobile lifestyle are both cultural and economic. If the husband is the sole or principal breadwinner, there are powerful economic incentives for a wife to adopt a mobile lifestyle, either to continue to make his breadwinning possible, or to enhance his earning capacity. Thus where the choice is between staying immobile with a lower standard of living or increasing it by moving around, the pressures are all upon the wife to accommodate herself to a mobile lifestyle, rather than deny a better standard of living not only to herself but also (and perhaps more powerfully) to her husband and children. This appears to have been well understood by the wives of highly mobile middle class families studied by Gaynor Cohen. She notes that 'most wives obviously recognised the connection between the demands of their husbands' jobs and their own financial needs and were prepared to accept mobility as a necessary evil' (Cohen, 1977, p. 599).

Of course, facilitating her husband's mobility need not always mean that the whole family has to move every time. But the choice to live separately again entails pressures which are both cultural and economic. In Farris's small study of ten couples adopting a 'commuting' lifestyle, the most commonly cited problem was the high financial cost of sustaining the pattern (Farris, 1978, p. 105). In some jobs, there is a direct financial incentive for a wife to live with her husband, and therefore to follow him when he moves. An interesting example of this can be found in the prison service, where not only is a prison officer entitled to superior quarters if he is married, but also elements in his pay are linked to the type of quarters which he occupies. This system of the Pensionable Value of Quarters means that officers in married quarters have additions made to their pension entitlement, and also have their overtime pay calculated at a higher rate. Thus these additional payments are made only if an officer is living 'in married circumstances', that is, if he has his wife living with him. If he is married but his wife lives elsewhere, he will forfeit the additional payment. This very specific instance provides an interesting example of an institutionalised incentive for a wife to live with her husband and to follow him when he moves.

The economic incentive fits well, of course, with the cultural norm that married couples live together. Stated in that form it sounds innocuous enough, but in practice it means that a wife goes wherever her husband is. This principle indeed was reflected in British law in the concept which prevailed until 1973, that a wife's legal domicile was that of her husband, even if they were separated. Indeed, a wife could find that she was legally domiciled in a country which she had never visited, nor ever intended to visit, if her husband deserted her and acquired a fresh domicile abroad (Bromley, 1976, p. 12).

The cultural imagery that a wife follows her husband wherever his work takes him is very significant, because it is centrally bound to images of what constitutes a good wife. Being prepared to follow one's husband is a sign of the helpmeet wife, who ideally should not only follow, but should do so selflessly, loyally and cheerfully. Such is the picture that emerges from an article in the magazine of the Soldiers, Sailors and Airmen's Families Association, whose author enthuses about the early RAF wives in the following terms: 'those loyal, single-minded and pioneer wives, who followed their husbands relentlessly, producing their babies with ill-timed enthusiasm in the most unlikely places, and camped under canvas' (Peelo, 1971, p. 9). Conversely, a wife who deliberately chooses to live separately from her husband in the course of her own work can apparently be expected to be treated as a deviant (Farris, 1978, p. 106), although perhaps she is less at risk if she is also dutifully bringing up his children.

The opportunities for a wife to resist a geographically mobile lifestyle therefore seem limited, should she wish to do so. Some women emphasise the positive features of being mobile. The Pahls found that some of their managers' wives claimed to like moving: they 'take pleasure in meeting new people, seeing new places and having a new house to arrange'; they 'find moving stimulating' and 'talk of being in a rut if they stay too long in one place' (Pahl and Pahl, 1971, p. 62). Undoubtedly women can experience some features of a mobile lifestyle as attractive; although it is difficult to interpret what 'liking' means if there is effectively no choice about whether to be mobile, as would be most clearly the case, say, in the armed forces. However, even where mobility is experienced as pleasurable in part, it remains true that it imposes a particular kind of structure over time upon the lives of women. Two specific features of this structure will now be considered: prospects for a wife's own employment, and her friendships.

Mortimer *et al.*, in reviewing the literature on wives' employment, conclude that such studies show that 'the family's geographic mobility is detrimental to the employed wife's continued labour force participation' and the 'likelihood of the wife's dropping out of the labour force is increased with the distance moved' (Mortimer, Hall and Hill, 1978, p. 302). The question of husband's mobility and a wife's employment should really be divided into three separate but linked questions: Does mobility effectively prevent wives obtaining *any* employment? Does mobility oblige wives to take *less desirable* employment? Does mobility mean that wives who are professionally trained and qualified are effectively prevented from developing a career line of their own?

The likelihood that a move will actually preclude a wife from finding employment obviously depends somewhat on local labour market conditions, as well as upon her skills. The most extreme cases of this probably occur when a husband's work takes him abroad. Diplomats' wives, for example, may find that they are prevented from working because of barriers to the employment of foreign nationals in the countries to which their husbands happen to have been posted. Wives of soldiers posted to the British Army of the Rhine reported great difficulty in finding employment of any sort, especially the wives of 'other ranks', who usually resorted to cleaning or catering work, often connected with the army itself. They attributed their employment difficulties in part specifically to mobility. There was, they said, 'an unwillingness on the part of employers to offer army wives jobs because of Army movement' (Ministry of Defence, 1976, para. 125). Officers' wives, however, 'were in general more able to continue in the kind of work for which they were both qualified and experienced' (ibid., para. 126). Army officers' wives may be more fortunate than other women: being able to find *appropriate* work is by no means the experience of all wives. Mortimer *et al.* conclude that the evidence suggests that there is a real possibility of the 'underemployment' of wives, especially those who are highly educated, who may be faced with the choice between unemployment, and work which does not utilise their skills (Mortimer, Hall and Hill, 1978, p. 302). This conclusion is certainly illustrated in the Pahls's work, where they note that 'Frequent moves mean that a wife has no opportunity of getting really experienced in one job and one area, and it severely limits the type of employment which she can take up' (Pahl and Pahl, 1971, p. 136). Where wives want to develop their own career line, the logistics of doing this in a tight employment market, whilst following one's husband around, are formidable. Even in balmier days, it was not necessarily easy: in the study of a 1960 cohort of graduates, Chisholm and Woodward found that changes in employment occasioned by their husbands' job moves had been a factor in one-quarter of women's labour force movements since graduation (Chisholm and Woodward, 1980, p. 173). Preliminary findings from a study of British women who graduated in 1965 and 1972 confirm that the demands of husband's (or partner's) job represent the single most important cause of household migration, and that 38 per cent of such women regarded such moves as 'damaging' to their own career development (Brzeskwinski, 1981, p. 7).

Little is known about the ways in which couples handle complexities of trying to pursue two careers, either or both of which may entail geographical mobility. What little is known suggests that the female partner is likely to be the more disadvantaged. Berger, Foster and Wallston's study of dual-career couples has shown that even where both partners actively seek to facilitate the wife's career, actual decisions about moves tend most often to favour the husband. Over half the couples they studied had developed job-seeking strategies which were initially egalitarian (operating on the basis that neither career was inherently more important than the other). However, when final decisions were made about a move, only a quarter were actually on an egalitarian basis: most decisions in the end reverted to the traditional strategy of wife following husband. This does not simply provide evidence about the strength of traditional cultural norms. The authors argue that this change was due as much to the operation of the labour market: the men got offered jobs more readily or more quickly than did the women, so the decision became a choice between accepting one job which one partner wanted, or letting it go with no knowledge of whether there was an alternative. Thus, the authors comment, 'given a tight job market in which men are more likely to get jobs, married women who strongly value their own careers may nevertheless end up following their husbands, despite the fact that they *are* as committed to their careers as their husbands are . . . they do not make the sacrifice readily, but under duress' (Berger, Foster and Wallston, 1978, p. 27).

So following a geographically mobile husband constrains a wife's life in that it means that she relinquishes a degree of control over her own employment prospects, which would be present if she were able to live where it best suited *her* chances of obtaining appropriate work. It also has the effect of obliging her to relinquish control over other aspects of her lifestyle, especially the development of social contacts (with kin, friends and acquaintances) over time.

Evidence that wives experience geographical mobility as highly disruptive of their friendships and other social contacts is apparent in studies of several occupational groups. Police wives report that they find frequent moves mean loss of friends (Whittaker, 1964, p. 125; Cain, 1973, p. 154), and army wives experienced difficulty in forming friendships with civilians (Ministry of Defence, 1976, para. 124).

It may be that the effect of moves upon friendships is more or less disruptive according to their frequency and their predictability. Uncertainty about the duration of a stay in a particular place, for example, may act as a disincentive to developing relationships there. Mitchell's postal survey of police wives in Scotland shows that 40 per cent of wives in the country areas felt that 'frequent moves militated against putting down roots in a place, making friends, joining local associations and, in general becoming integrated into an area' (Mitchell, 1975, p. 83).

The logistics of developing new sets of friends at frequent intervals are resolved by some people by effectively restricting their orbit to others in like situations. Thus one of the respondents in Bell's study says:

> I have found now that the majority of my friends also work for the same company . . . and my wife is only really friendly with the wives of my colleagues. This I suppose is yet another reason for not leaving the company.   (Bell, 1968, p. 32)

Cohen has provided a very useful account of a group of mobile middle class wives on a suburban housing estate, whose network of friendships and practical support constituted what she calls a 'distinctive subculture' (Cohen, 1977, p. 595). This pattern of relationships enabled them to replace some of the supportive relationships which they probably would have found elsewhere if they had not been mobile: 'Through co-operation on the estate, the majority managed to obtain the kind of help which others received from their kin' (ibid., p. 599).

Examples of successful re-creation of friendships in a variety of circumstances notwithstanding, the process of doing this is likely to be problematic for all but a small minority. Partly this is a matter of social skills, which not all women possess in equal measure. The Pahls note that managers' wives whose own background was working class were less likely to seek out friends in a new area (Pahl and Pahl, 1971, p. 155); and, writing of the sample as a whole, they observe: 'for many, moving house means making new friends, an operation which may be associated with anxiety or anticipation or satisfaction, as old conceptions of herself are confirmed or found unacceptable, new ones revealed, and new patterns of relationships worked out' (Pahl and Pahl, 1971, p. 153). The association of the making of friendships with central aspects of personal identity makes it a particularly hazardous business, depending as it does on complex interpersonal negotiations on the basis of what Allan has called 'implicit rules of relevance' (Allan, 1979, pp. 12–18). Nicholson's interesting study of friendships among wives on a naval housing estate, who mostly live a very mobile lifestyle, illustrated the essential precariousness of the process. She observes: 'Many made friends very quickly on the estate and regretted it afterwards, as new relationships were often overloaded too soon

with misplaced confidences, and withdrawn loneliness often the result'
(Nicholson, 1980, p. 59).

So geographical mobility occasioned by a man's work can structure his
wife's life in ways central to her employment prospects, her lifestyle
and her personal identity. For the male worker, the mobile lifestyle
has an inherent thread of continuity, precisely because each move is
related to his work. For his wife, however, as a secondary participant
in this process, there is inherent disruption rather than continuity. In
so far as mobility entails, as Seidenberg puts it, difficulties in
transferring personal credentials from one location to another
(Seidenberg, 1973, p. 10), a wife who does seek to impose some kind of
personal coherence upon a mobile lifestyle in which she is only a
vicarious participant will have poor materials with which to work.

Special Case: Home as Workbase

Although the experience of a small minority, the use of the home as
the husband's workbase has particular significance for this study, since
it provides some especially clear examples of how the organisation of a
man's work structures his wife's life. Also, it will be argued in Part
Two, it offers special opportunities for a wife to be drawn into his
work.

Despite the argument that a major feature of industrialisation was to
produce a separation between the two, plenty of examples can be
found where the home provides the sole or the major workbase.
Publicans, clergy, policemen and farmers commonly live where they
work; and owners of small businesses, self-employed craftsmen,
freelance writers and journalists commonly work *from* home, even if
work sometimes takes place elsewhere. In addition, many other
people use the home as a *partial* workbase: senior managers, civil
servants, teachers, academics and many others commonly bring work
home, sometimes using the home 'almost like a branch office' (Young
and Willmott, 1973, p. 136).

Home-based work both allows the worker more control over his or
her own schedules than is afforded by many other work settings, and
changes the character of the relationship between work and non-work.
It blurs the distinction between work and non-work *time* (see above,
pp. 26–31), between work and non-work *space* and between work and
non-work *activities*. The greater apparent autonomy which this affords
may be cherished as a part of high status work. Young and Willmott
found that work was almost never done at home by the manual
workers in their sample, but more commonly by the self-employed and
those who could 'exercise their autonomy by not turning up at their

office if they wished' (Young and Willmott, 1973, p. 168). However, the apparent autonomy may prove illusory if the result is that work takes over completely. That possibility is all too evident in the perceptive study of small shopkeepers by Bechhofer *et al.*, where work can take over the whole family.

> The insidious ways in which business matters intrude upon the lives of family members are not hard to imagine, but in some cases we find our respondents pointing to an important paradox. Autonomy has turned to serfdom. The owner and his family are bound to the shop; the enterprise stands over and above them and that which was to guarantee a new freedom has brought instead a new alienation . . . The long hours, the isolation and the involvement of other family members means that the sharp division customarily made between 'work' and 'non-work' is in this instance hard to draw.
> (Bechhofer, Elliott, Rushforth and Bland, 1974b, p. 479)

That serfdom has a particular character for wives who, quite literally, 'live over the shop' in which they also work, because it offers them the dubious privilege of combining domestic work with labour (not necessarily paid) in the family business. This is illustrated by a study of French bakers, where husbands do the baking, and wives are the shopkeepers:

> [Bakers' wives] have to keep the shop open from eight in the morning . . . to eight in the evening, sometimes without interruption . . . To do this work as a shopkeeper six days a week – work which by the way gives no salary, no social rights whatsoever, and no property right either – they must add the work of housewife and mother.   (Bertaux and Bertaux-Wiame, 1981, p. 163)

The blurring of distinctions of time, space and activities varies somewhat with the character and organisation of the work. Probably the most extreme cases of blurring are those where it is sometimes unclear whether an activity *counts* as work or not. Is a doctor who watches a medical programme on television working or not? Is the social scientist's careful daily reading of the newspapers work or not? When the blurring of activities is combined with the blurring of distinctions of time and space, then work really can pervade one's whole life.

Since working at home gives work a particular structure and character, what implications does this have for the worker's wife – whether or not she is in employment herself? It will be argued that the two main ways in which this structures her life are: first, household space and household routines get organised around the male breadwinner's work needs; secondly, the home becomes reconstituted as a semi-public place.

Household routines can be organised around the breadwinner's work needs even when work takes place outside the home. However, when work is done *at* home, an additional dimension is introduced: domestic organisation can directly either facilitate or impair the worker's ability actually to do the work. Especially if the worker-at-home is the sole or main family breadwinner, there is a powerful case for organising family routines and activities around his working needs. This case is no less powerful if the worker works at home only sometimes, since in many cases work may be brought home precisely *because* this is thought to provide a setting where uninterrupted work can take place. In Young and Willmott's study of managers, two in every five had worked at home during the week before the interview, sometimes staying at home in order to concentrate on jobs which they could do better there (Young and Willmott, 1973, p. 168).

It is one thing to say that home provides a suitable setting for concentrated work when one lives alone; but when one shares one's home with others, including perhaps young children, then special arrangements need to be made if it is to provide a peaceful haven. At this point, enter the wife. In most cases, it will probably fall to her to create a domestic setting suitable for work. Glastonbury gives some interesting illustrations of this in her lively article about the domestic arrangements of great writers, in which she argues that 'the poet depends upon manual labour at home – usually female – and upon which he confers the blessing of his own uniqueness' (Glastonbury, 1978, p. 30). She recommends some pertinent questions with which to confront great productions of literature:

> It may be useful to confront literary achievement with the challenge that the worker in Brecht's poem brought to the Great Names of History:
>
> > Someone wins on every page
> > Who cooked the winner's banquet?
>
> Yes indeed: 'Did you do it all by yourself? How many hot dinners, how many changes of shirt, how many delegated chores, make a book?' (ibid., p. 29)

In their introduction to the same publication, Flynn and Davidoff use the fascinating illustration of the domestic organisation of the Durkheim household, drawing upon Lukes's account. Lukes only mentions MrsDurkheim once, they note, but her organisation of the home was clearly crucial to the production of his writings:

His marriage . . . could not have been happier, both personally and in creating an atmosphere conducive to his work . . . Mauss writes . . . that his wife 'created for him the respectable and quiet family existence which he considered the best guarantee of morality and of life. She removed from him every material care and all frivolity and for his sake took charge of the education of Marie and Andre Durkheim'.

(Flynn and Davidoff, 1978, pp. 5–6, quoting Lukes, 1973)

An academic's wife, one of Fowlkes's respondents, illustrates the same process in a contemporary setting:

I feel somewhat restricted as to what I can do in the house when he works here. I can't listen to music in the morning . . . Also he doesn't like babysitters here. When he's working intensively he likes a quiet house and doesn't want to have to worry about it . . . *My husband's work needs define our routines here.*

(Fowlkes, 1980, p. 104) (my italics)

Having one's husband working at home is not simply a matter of organising household routines in a different way, but it actually generates more work. As one clergyman's wife in my study put it,

The house is constantly being used, it never stays just done. Another big thing is meals, because you've to provide a meal obviously at every meal-time; whereas if two people are out, they can eat out at midday; you might even have your main meal out, and then you wouldn't have to worry about it in the evenings. Whereas if they are in at lunchtime, which they usually are, then you've got to provide a meal, and that's an extra worry, an extra thing to organise'

(Spedding, 1975, p. 288)

The implications of having one's husband working at home are clearly far reaching for the wife who takes the role of household manager. One possible way of avoiding this, at least in part, might be to work full-time outside the home oneself. But this does not necessarily change fundamentally a wife's role in organising the home as a congenial work setting for her husband. One of the few clergymen's wives in my study who did go out to work (she worked as a full-time primary school teacher) recorded in the diary which she kept for me a pattern of daily living in which she organised the home as a fit working place for her husband, before she went to school and after she came home. The following day is quite typical of this respondent's diary:

Day: Monday
    Got up at: 7.30

Morning:
7.30 to 8.30	Prepared husband's lunch and pre-set it in cooker. Breakfast
8.30 to 12.00	At school
Lunch at 12.30	(on duty)

Afternoon:
1.00 to 4.00	At school
4.00 to 4.30	Cup of tea and crossword
4.30 to 5.30	Cleaned landing and stairs and washed down all the paintwork. Prepared tea.
Evening meal at: 6.00	

Evening:
7.00 to 9.30	Weekly ironing
9.30 to 10.30	Watched TV and discussed church cleaning for tomorrow
Went to bed at: 11.00	

The round of domestic work still took place when this wife *was* at home: going out to work simply meant that she got up earlier in the mornings to arrange her husband's lunch before she left.

A wife's organisation of the home around the needs of the worker is not merely faithful adherence to cultural prescription: there is clearly an economic dimension. Just as it was argued that wives have little choice but to follow a geographically mobile husband if their long-term livelihood depends on his work, so too there is a powerful logic in the argument that the worker-at-home must not be too distracted by domestic concerns and must be given optimum working conditions. The logic works best if a wife is economically dependent upon her husband – perhaps works less well if she is not.

The second important feature of the use of the home as husband's workbase is that the home becomes a kind of public place. The most obvious instances of this are where the male breadwinner uses the house for seeing clients, sales representatives, and so on: people who have come to see him directly 'on business', probably by pre-arranged appointment. Such visits involve the intrusion of strangers into the domestic setting, but wives probably experience these as the least disruptive of public intrusions, since they occur at predictable times. More disruptive, because of their unpredictability, are the kinds of continuous visits on minor matters which lead clergy wives to say they feel that their home is constantly 'on view', as do policeman's wives, who reported to Mitchell that living in a police house means 'loss of family privacy, since people called upon their husband's services even when he was off duty'. As one wife wrote,

> Home life is continuously disrupted. Children awakened at night with the doorbell and telephone. Mealtimes interrupted even when there are visitors in the house.   (Mitchell, 1975, p. 83)

Wives of the clergy perhaps provide the most extreme example of a home being on view, since the use of their home in the course of their husbands' work is not confined to a room designated as his study, but often extends to the use of the family sitting-room for meetings of all sorts (Spedding, 1975, ch. 12). Certainly, there are other occupations in which the home is used for work-related gatherings, especially the use of 'official residences' of politicians and diplomats. But there one would not expect the ambassador's wife to have cleaned the house before the party's arrival, nor that any lapses in housekeeping standards would be automatically laid at her door, as would usually be the case for wives of the clergy, who are put in the position not only of having their home used as a public place, but of feeling that they are held accountable for its appearance. The particular pressures to produce a suitably clean and tidy house derive from the possibility that one's husband's position, as well as one's own, will be undermined if domestic appearances are not kept up: in some jobs, he may lose status as a public figure, in others it would, quite simply, be bad for business.

The constitution of the home as a semi-public place through its use as a workbase is certainly experienced by wives as an intrusion: they use phrases like being 'on view' or 'loss of privacy'. However, in terms of the present analysis, its particular interest is that it shows that domestic settings cannot always be regarded as solely 'the private domain'. Where work is based in the home, the home is part of the 'public' domain, both structurally and experientially, and the notion that there is a clear distinction between the two is called into question. At the same time, wives' expressions of dissatisfaction, and the very fact that they do experience it as intrusion, underline the strength of the ideology that the home *should* constitute a completely private domain.

Special Case: Tied Accommodation

Tied accommodation is discussed here because it is an example of the spatial location of the home in relation to a husband's work, which has rather special implications for wives. Those implications are: first, that a wife relinquishes aspects of control over her home to her husband's employer; secondly, that she becomes identified with his work through her occupation of that home.

Although a minority experience, tied housing can be found in quite a wide range of occupations. Burke has recently listed these as including: nurses, teachers, au pairs, domestic servants, servicemen, hotel and bar staff, caretakers, prison officers, firemen, policemen, ambulancemen, clergymen, coalminers, council gravediggers, some employees of the British Steel Corporation, as well as agricultural and forestry commission workers (Burke, 1981, pp. 99–100). The largest number of tied dwellings is in agriculture, followed closely by the mining industry (Constable, 1974, p. 25). The type of accommodation provided can be very diverse: from the stereotypical agricultural worker's cottage to some very grand 'official residences' occupied by members of the diplomatic corps and politicians, not to mention the royal family.

Whatever the balance of advantages and disadvantages from the point of view of the worker, the provision of tied accommodation is, in most cases, clearly in the interests of the employer. The movement of military personnel, and indeed the maintenance of military authority, would be virtually impossible without tied accommodation for soldiers themselves. Indeed, the mobility of the workforce is a fairly common rationale for its provision – in the diplomatic service, the police and the church, for example. The traditional rationale for providing agricultural labourers with tied housing was that the need to find their own accommodation in the relevant area would be a serious barrier to recruitment. The more positive side of the same theme is that potential employees do sometimes find the prospect of a house attractive. In two case studies of British Rail resident railway crossing keepers undertaken for the Low Pay Unit, both families gave needing a house because of a wife's pregnancy as a major reason for taking the job (Owen, 1980, pp. 15–19). The utility of tied housing for recruitment is as theme which emerges in relation to other occupations which attract predominantly young male working class recruits, although this can be problematic if it is successful, since most employers want workers to be attracted to the *job*, not just to the house. An editorial in the *SAAFA Magazine*, commenting in 1963 on a decision to accept no more married men as recruits, berated the latter because 'far too many married men [have] been joining the army *for no better reason* than that it seemed to be the only way of getting a house' (*SAAFA Magazine*, April 1963, p. 1) (my italics).

A key feature built into the structure of the tied accommodation system is that employer–employee relationships become tangled with those of landlord and tenant. This has two interesting implications, which are of equal importance for the worker and his wife. First, in many cases, there is a structured ambiguity about whether the provision of tied accommodation provides an element of pay. If the worker lives rent-free, or at lower than the economic rent, the accommodation does provide part of the remuneration associated with the job. The May Committee on the prison service was clearly irritated that prison officers failed to be suitably grateful for this: 'One of the most valuable elements in the remuneration of prison service grades is the provision of free housing . . . despite that, among the most frequent complaints which we have heard . . . have been those concerning the subject of quarters' (*Committee of Inquiry into the United Kingdom Prison Services*, 1979, para. 11.4). The provision of any tied accommodation as an element of pay effectively removes the choice of where to live even if that choice formally exists, because to decline it implies a reduction in pay. Secondly, occupying tied accommodation puts a worker in a situation where the employer has a greater hold over him or her, since decisions about one's home as well as one's work are taken by the employer. In the last resort, putting one's job at risk also means putting one's home at risk. In some occupations this power is given effectively to hierarchical superiors. In Cain's study, one-third of the city police wives 'were anxious for a fairly immediate move, and of course dependent upon senior officers to provide this' (Cain, 1973, p. 159), and the delicacy of the relationships was well recognised by one of her male police subjects who commented,

> So long as you're in one of their houses you've lost that bit of independence and they've always got that over you.
>
> (ibid., p. 159)

An additional hazard from a wife's point of view is that her husband's death or desertion often, although not inevitably, may mean that she also loses her home. Press reports of the suicide in 1980 of a wife of a former Buckingham Palace employee were quick to make the connection that the woman had lost her right to live in her flat at St James's Palace after her husband had left her (*Guardian*, 6 September 1980).

Complaints about tied accommodation often refer to the quality and suitability of the premises, and lack of opportunity to undertake home improvements. Cain found that more than half the rural police wives in her study were dissatisfied with their present house or its condition (Cain, 1973, p. 158), and one of her respondents elaborated on her complaints:

> There's this house. I must admit I'm disappointed about that. I'd

been looking forward to a house and that. And then the cooker came, and I was ashamed that anyone should see it coming in the door. It's an old thing with bent legs you know. The man came up to put a new hotplate in, and he said it would be cheaper for the police force to buy a new one . . . there's horrible old lino in the hall and no carpet . . . The upstairs is so damp. The water was running down the walls this winter.   (Cain, unpublished data)

The worker dependent on tied accommodation effectively is put in the situation where he must take what he is given. From the point of view of the wife, the crucial point about this is that it removes from her any real possibility of participation in decisions quite fundamental to her lifestyle, and puts them into the hands of her husband's employer. These are decisions about where she shall live, and the character and the quality of accommodation of the housing she shall occupy. They also include matters which may seem trivial, but create quite widespread irritation among wives in tied housing. In Mitchell's survey of police wives, the most common cause of complaint was about the rule that prevented the occupants from decorating or making structural alterations (Mitchell, 1975, p. 82), plus complaints about the non-standardisation of fittings, so that carpets, curtains, and so on, could never be transferred from one house to the next (ibid., p. 83). The May Report noted prison officers' dissatisfaction with reported long delays in carrying out repairs and redecorations, but adds loftily: 'many of these matters are the inevitable consequences of the provided quarters system' (*Committee of Inquiry into the United Kingdom Prison Services*, 1979, para. 11.19). In some occupations, wives even lose any control over the choice of furnishings and other household items, since the tied accommodation is also furnished. This applies to diplomats, for example, and also to the services. The other side of relinquishing control over the contents of one's home is that a wife's standards of housekeeping and household maintenance are potentially visible to her husband's employer: he owns the contents of her house, and she may ultimately be called to account for her stewardship of them. One RAF wife has described this, in suitably military tones:

We 'marched in' to an all-furnished home. The contents of the house were held, as they are now, in inventory – against the Day of Reckoning, the 'marching out' . . . Damage to equipment was a major catastrophe.   (Peelo, 1971, p. 9)

Nicholson's more recent study on a naval housing estate confirms that wives are responsible for the contents of their quarters, and when they are moving they will be subject to a 'muster out', that is, checking the inventory of household furniture and furnishings originally allocated to them (Nicholson, 1980, p. 28). The process of relinquishing control over decisions in the domestic sphere can happen even when the tied accommodation goes with a very élite job. Margaret Jay, in an interview about being married to the British Ambassador in Washington, very clearly accepted that decisions about her home were really out of her hands:

> If London decided . . . that they would prefer Peter and I and the children to live in a much smaller house, or in an apartment, where we just lived as a family, and couldn't have large numbers of people to stay, then I wouldn't mind . . . that in a sense is a policy decision to be taken in London; that's not something over which I have discretion. (Jay, 1977)

Tied accommodation structures and limits a wife's choices in the domestic sphere; it also often has the effect of conferring upon her a vicarious, 'wife of' identity badge. The wife who lives in the house known to be the residence of the local vicar or policeman will find it very difficult to escape being identified by her husband's work. Where work is hierarchically organised, tied accommodation not only acts as a badge of vicarious occupational identity, but also as a badge of vicarious rank for a wife. Prison officers occupy 'major' or 'minor' quarters according to rank, for example, and similar systems occur in most hierarchically organisational settings. Mitchell notes this for the police: 'In the country area, each posting carried its own house, so that any change in the man's job (e.g. from village policeman to C.I.D. or promotion to uniform duties in a larger station) meant a change of house also' (Mitchell, 1975, p. 82). Within the hierarchy of the Church of England, exactly the same applies: a curate's house is almost always quite distinct from a vicar's house, and usually smaller, while a bishop's house is somewhat grander, as indicated by its traditional designation as 'bishop's palace'.

So the occupation of tied accommodation closely circumscribes a wife's domestic circumstances, and often her public identity. It is of course the experience of only a minority of wives, and represents a degree of incorporation into one's husband's work, and a lifestyle structured by it, which is a comparatively rare experience. Nevertheless, the existence of such instances, across quite a wide range of occupational settings, demonstrates a very significant degree of structuring of wives' lives can be accepted, and its legitimacy remain largely unquestioned.

Special Case: Institutional Settings

The organisation of certain types of work opens up the possibility for incorporating wives into an institutional setting. This incorporation can be partial or all-embracing. Examples of all-embracing incorporation are found where wives live physically within the confines of an institution such as an army camp or a boarding school, and these are often associated with tied housing. Partial incorporation can occur in a much wider range of occupations, when wives accompany their husbands to a variety of official occasions, social events, or trips abroad.

The location of wives in an institutional setting is obviously a special case (Papanek, 1973, p. 859), but of interest because of the opportunities it affords for incorporating wives in an explicit and detailed way. The most extreme examples are where lives are lived almost totally within the confines of the institution, which from a wife's point of view means that the structures of daily life are laid down in some detail by her husband's employer. Writing of American military camps, Dobrofsky and Batterson describe this:

> Wives are particularly insulated by military services, which accommodate every need and which are immediately available to them . . . at reduced prices. Military families can shop, drink, dance, attend movies, parties and planned trips at all times and at lower costs than civilians necessarily pay for the same items and activities. The conveniences in time, energy and expense might make anyone take advantage of them.
> (Dobrofsky and Batterson, 1977, p. 676)

This neatly illustrates how employers' provision for the needs of families in an institutional setting can be double-edged. Goods and services provided more cheaply are economically advantageous to wives; but at the same time, the fact that almost everything they need is provided by their husbands' employer means that wives are drawn more closely into the institutional structure. That is reinforced of course by the physical isolation of many of these highly structured institutional settings. But similar patterns may occur on a more temporary basis for those wives who are incorporated into the institutional structures of their husbands' work only from time to time. The particular ways in which such settings impose structures upon wives will be considered under two main headings: being subject to institutional definitions of appropriate behaviour; and having one's social relationships structured through incorporation in the institutional hierarchy.

Although many employers may have notions about what constitutes a suitable wife for their employees, the significance of institutional settings is that they make a wife much more *visible*, and therefore more vulnerable to having her suitability measured against the notional ideal. In the past, it was regarded by some employers as quite legitimate for them to have views on potential marriage partners. This was certainly the case in the army, where officers (but, interestingly enough, not other ranks) used to have to obtain approval of their prospective brides from their commanding officer (Bamfield, 1975, p. 20), and it was commonly the custom in the Church of England that the clergy should introduce their fiancées to the diocesan bishop (Spedding, 1975, ch. 15). Although there appear to be no contemporary examples where this kind of vetting is formalised and explicit, that is no guarantee that such vetting does not continue in a more informal way, although the sanctions may be different. Although it may simply be presented as a friendly and welcoming move, the invitation, say, for a prospective political candidate, or a clergyman viewing a potential new parish, to 'bring your wife along' is the contemporary equivalent. It is difficult to believe that, in those circumstances, notions about a wife's suitability are not being formulated. Baker observes that much of the information available about the 'personalities and interests' of executives' wives was culled at 'informal' gatherings whose overt purpose was something else (Baker, 1976, p. 344).

Ideas about what constitutes a suitable wife for a man in a particular occupation can still exist even if they are not made explicit, and sometimes they relate quite specifically to her ability to support the job which he does. The church leaders expect that clergymen's wives at least should be committed Christians themselves, and be as active in the church as any other church member (Spedding, 1975, ch. 15). Corporation officials, according to Whyte, regarded the ideal wife as someone who was highly adaptable, highly gregarious and realised that her husband really belonged to the corporation (Whyte, 1971, p. 79). A suitable diplomat's wife apparently is someone given to good works and community involvement, *inter alia*. Callan says that in her spare time she is ideally involved in charitable activities, especially fund-raising, which utilise women's traditional skills: 'commitment to voluntary work of this kind, together with "official duties" is perceived as an intrinsic part of the wife's identity; the role of the Embassy wife poses as it were, an *ex officio* moral content' (Callan, 1975, p. 96).

Perhaps the most significant feature of this is the assumption that it is entirely legitimate for an employer to have views about the wives of employees. Baker notes that most of the American companies in his study assumed that they had the right to judge wives' suitability living overseas, and one firm even administered psychological tests to wives

(Baker, 1976, p. 344). It is interesting to note that this is not necessarily matched by an equivalent level of responsibility *to* wives: only 68 per cent of wives, as compared with 84 per cent of male employees, were given pre-departure training. In some institutional settings, employers may claim the right not only to have views upon, but also to control, certain aspects of a wife's lifestyle. Callan argues that, despite recent changes of policy on diplomats' wives taking their own employment when abroad, these have 'left untouched the underlying principle: that in this area, the Administration claims an uncompromising authority over its employees wives' (Callan, 1975, p. 97).

The second major way in which institutional settings structure wives' lives is by incorporating them into the institutional hierarchy, and defining their position within it vicariously, according to their husbands' status. The consequence is that social relationships have to be handled within the structures imposed by those institutional definitions. The potential for doing this is greater the more totally a wife is located in the institutional setting. Where she lives physically within the confines of the institution, there is a good chance that the accommodation she occupies will act as a badge of vicarious rank. In those settings, there is the possibility of developing a formalised and highly structured pattern of social relationships based on vicarious rank, from which it must be very difficult to break free. Wakeford noted, in his study of a public boarding school, that 'the wives of staff share aspects of their husband's status' and notes that wives of housemasters have a status slightly superior to other wives (Wakeford, 1969, p. 163). Military settings provide another good example. A correspondent in 1957 to the *SAAFA Magazine*, writing about her experiences of being The Colonel's Lady (*sic*), gives the following illustration: 'It is heart-warming to be told by *Mrs Colour-Sergeant Richmond* that she remembers me coming down the aisle as a bride – "and real lovely you were too, ma'am"' (*SAAFA Magazine*, 1959, p. 73) (my italics). Quaint though this exchange may sound now, it is an excellent illustration of the way in which, at least not so very long ago, army wives routinely related to each other in terms of their husbands' rank. Since then, however, the *SAAFA Magazine* has contained a number of articles and letters on this topic, especially in relation to the activity of 'visiting' of the wives of other ranks by officers' wives. Some army wives take the view that the assumptions of rank expressed in this practice are inappropriate: 'I think that officers' wives nowadays must divest themselves of their lingering consciousness of rank – and few young women want to be "visited" however unpatronisingly it is done' (*SAAFA Magazine*, January 1967, p. 8).

The assumptions of vicarious rank can on occasions extend to the giving and taking of orders between wives. Callan, writing of her own experience as a diplomat's wife, says:

> An ambassador will frequently issue instructions to his staff and their wives; and his wife, in matters that concern the social life of the embassy, is fully entitled to do the same . . . it often happens that I am asked to do something by another wife, in the tone of one giving friendly instructions, where no formal relationship exists between us beyond the fact that her husband is a senior colleague of my husband.   (Callan, 1975, p. 91)

In Callan's view, diplomats' wives are often fairly ambivalent about their vicarious rank since 'one part of the wives' self-image defines them as people who do not take too seriously the rank differentials existing among their husbands' (ibid., p. 92). But on the other hand, the diplomatic service provides one of the clearest illustrations of incorporation into rank, since it happens in a very formal way: 'the principle that the wife of a diplomat is absorbed into her husband's role, sharing his rank and immunities, is built into protocol' (ibid., p. 89). Presumably, this means, at the very least, that significant departures from a pattern of relationships congruent with rank are very difficult to handle. The delicacy of handling relationships which depart from rank is illustrated when one party's vicarious rank changes. An example of this is provided by one of the studies of the police, where wives living in a colony of police houses find that 'There are problems of rank, embarrassments when friends get promoted, which the wives feel more keenly than the men since they have no accepted pattern of behaviour to follow in this situation' (Whittaker, 1964, p. 132). Several of Cain's respondents expressed hostility to such ghetto living precisely because of the operation of rank distinctions; for example:

> I've never lived in a police colony, thank God. Bloody awful places they are too. The thing is, policemen talk all the time, they're like that. And you find the wives take on rank more than the men do.
> (Cain, unpublished data)

Patterns of relationships based on vicarious rank are not confined to isolated institutional setting. Fowlkes's study shows that wives of academics traditionally were slotted into a shadow hierarchy within the faculty, which meant, for example, that newly arrived wives were taken under the wing of the department chairman's wife, and guided through suitably wifely concerns such as settling their children in school, or getting to know the local shops (Fowlkes, 1980, p. 63).

There is the potential for relationships based on vicarious rank every time wives meet each other in a setting which is in some way related to their husbands' work: at conferences, dinners, fêtes, or in those interesting organisations – wives' clubs. These exist in a variety of settings – the army, the diplomatic service, universities and the church. Whether or not they are located in institutionalised living arrangements, they derive their rationale from vicarious identification with one's husband's work, and therefore it is hardly surprising if vicarious rank forms the basis for their operation. In my study, about half of the anglican clergymen's wives attended clergy wives' meetings at least occasionally, and about one-third attended regularly. At the time of the study, these meetings were organised by the 'senior' clergyman's wife in the diocese – the bishop's wife, or a suitable substitute if the bishop was a bachelor. My own participant observation, along with wives' comments, led me to the view that these were primarily status-confirming rather than mutually supportive events, and relationships certainly were based upon vicarious rank. My own and several other people's observations confirmed that it is the practice in a number of dioceses to suggest that each wife wears a label on these occasions, indicating her name and 'where she comes from'. This means that she writes the name of her husband's church, thus enabling her to be vicariously ranked with the informal status hierarchy of parishes. I have even seen the graduations indicated more finely than that, with labels which say something to the effect 'Margaret Jones – curate at St Bartholemew's' – a patent but fascinating absurdity (Spedding, 1975, p. 379). A similar phenomenon is reported by Callan who, writing about the elections in 1970 for the Diplomatic Service Wives' Association, notes that candidates were listed on the ballot paper each with her husband's grade (Callan, 1975, p. 90). The rationale for this was that it would ensure the spread of nominees across a range of grades – a rationale which only serves to confirm that the wives were being defined primarily in terms of their husbands' status.

Institutional settings do in one sense provide rather special examples of structures being imposed upon wives, although where they operate they clearly leave very little room for manoeuvre. It can be argued, however, that they are special situations only in the sense of providing special *opportunities* for the processes of structuring to be expressed in clearly visible ways. Much of what goes on in these special settings often can be seen in more diffuse forms elsewhere, since the processes involved derive fundamentally from the organisation of work and of marriage in our society.

5

Constraints, Identities and Room for Manoeuvre

Developing Coping Strategies

What room for manoeuvre does a wife have, both within and around the structures which her husband's work imposes upon her? Supposing that she wants to establish a greater degree of control over her own life, will she find it possible?

To address these questions properly, it is necessary to bring together the various features so far which have been kept analytically distinct. We need to look at the ways in which the *overlapping* constraints imposed by a husband's working location, his hours of work, the character of his job, and so on, can combine to produce the complex patterns within and around which an individual wife will have to manoeuvre. Such complexities can perhaps best be illustrated by considering two contrasting cases, one where there seems very little room for manoeuvre, the other where there is apparently somewhat more.

In the discussion of hours of work, it was suggested that one of the most difficult work timetables for a wife to 'fit round' was where the worker has a high degree of discretion about when the work is done. This is compounded when that work is normally based in the home – a situation which, again it has been argued, is of particular significance for a wife. In the case of wives of the clergy, those two elements combine with a third – the highly valued 'moral' content of the work of a husband who is a public figure – to produce a situation which leaves wives with very little room for manoeuvre indeed. What would be a contrasting case, which leaves more space for wives? The key features here seem to be regularity and predictability of working hours, combined with a job which cannot be 'brought home' and is non-contaminating. The wife of an office worker, for example, or a factory worker who works completely regular shifts, may have the most chance of organising her life in a way which leaves her some degree of personal control, especially if she can rely on her husband to undertake child care outside working hours.

Regular availability of one's husband is not, however, an essential precondition of establishing a degree of control over one's life. Indeed, it may be something of a mixed blessing, since his very presence increases domestic demands. Consider, by contrast, the situation of wives whose husbands' work takes them away from home for periods of time, either regularly or irregularly – to sea, on an oil rig, or travelling in Britain and abroad. In these circumstances especially, wives are left with sole responsibility for the domestic scene for periods of the year. What kind of structures does that particular pattern impose on them?

One might imagine that it could be very difficult for a wife to take work in these circumstances, since her husband is not available on a *regular* basis as a substitute. Tunstall's study of deep-sea fishermen showed that very few fishermen's wives were in employment except episodically (Tunstall, 1962, p. 161). Hollowell notes that the wives of long-distance lorry drivers dislike their husbands' irregular working hours, but he does not link that specifically with their own employment opportunities (Hollowell, p. 153).

Although one's husband's periodic absences do impose a very particular kind of pattern upon a wife's life, and oblige her to take total responsibility for his home and children, there is actually some evidence that this particular pattern may be one where it is *easier* to devise coping strategies, precisely because one's husband is sometimes completely out of the way. In these circumstances, wives are freer to devise strategies to meet the needs of their children and themselves, without having to take account of a husband's working timetable on a day-to-day basis. The strategies which they devise typically exclude him altogether. Hollowell notes that long-distance lorry drivers' wives are likely to 'develop a certain amount of self-sufficiency, and to regard the husband as something external. This is shown by the fact that drivers say that their wives' domestic routines are actually disturbed by their irregular times of returning home' (ibid., p. 155). Cohen's (1977) study of a middle class housing estate where husbands are frequently absent from home offers an interesting account of the ways in which wives are able to develop very satisfactory coping strategies, in this case on a neighbourly basis, presumably on the principle that all are in the same boat.

A pattern of work which takes a husband away from home of course may not be welcomed by either husband or wife for a variety of reasons. Hollowell paints a picture of lorry drivers apparently trying to elbow their way back into family life, and going to what he regards as excessive lengths in order to do so: 'The husband attempts to compensate his wife and family for his absence by a more intensive effort to organise and give companionship when he does return at weekends. Some drivers *took this to extremes* by doing the household cleaning and cooking the meals' (Hollowell, 1968, pp. 162–3) (my italics). Wives of lorry drivers also dislike their husbands' absences, fearing especially the opportunities for sexual adventures (ibid.), and soldiers' wives complained of feeling isolated and lonely, and having greater difficulties with their children when their husband is away (Ministry of Defence, 1976, paras 138–9). The notion that periodic separations constitute a culturally 'abnormal' family situation accounts for the dislike of it, at least in part. But whatever its disadvantanges on other grounds, it seems the way it structures a wife's life leaves her with somewhat more control over her own life than many other wives experience, despite appearances to the contrary.

Thus it seems that, for a wife who wants to develop satisfactory coping strategies for fitting her life around her husband's work, the best deal probably is either to have a husband whose work takes him completely away from home, or one who works hours which are totally regular and predictable (provided he can be co-opted as a substitute for her in the home). The circumstance which perhaps initially appears most auspicious – having a husband who can organise his own working hours and can work at home – turns out if anything to be the most constraining from a wife's point of view.

The Social Location of a Wife

What a man 'does' defines his status, but whom she marries defines a woman's. In meeting strangers, one can 'place' a man socially by asking what he does, a woman by asking what her husband does.
(Rossi, 1971, p. 110)

This very apposite observation of Alice Rossi's forms the organising theme of this final section. The extent to which a woman is defined socially by her husband's work has been illustrated in a number of different ways in this chapter: the level of material provision which his job offers is a major determinant of her lifestyle; some women are closely identified with their husbands' work by living in a house owned by his employer; some by being incorporated in an occupational hierarchy, or by being given a vicarious public figure identity. However, the specific point about social status perhaps deserves some further examination.

The implicit sexism in the practice of categorising women's social class by the occupation of their husbands has been recognised for some time. Acker's key article (1973) has been very influential in exposing the underlying contradictions in this practice, but it remains one of the ways in which sociology often mirrors the assumptions which it is supposed to be studying (Oakley, 1974b, ch. 1). Although there is no excuse for this assumption remaining unquestioned by sociologists, the practice of designating a woman's social status via her husband's occupation does reflect cultural processes which are very real in their consequences.

The major cultural assumption which is exposed is that wives relate to the real world – that is to say, the public domain, as defined and created by men – in a second-hand way. Safilios-Rothschild has examined this in relation to American sociology of the family, and argues that the traditional view is that each family has one main 'linkage' to the outside world, and that this is provided by the husband's job; if there is more than one linkage, the lines get crossed, so to speak (Safilios-Rothschild, 1976, p. 51).

To put the same kind of point within the conceptual framework already employed in this chapter: *all* wives, not only those of men in 'public figure' occupations, have a vicarious identity conferred upon them through marriage, and it is one from which probably they cannot escape, even if it becomes overlaid with additional identities which they acquire in their own right. However, one consequence of having one's major status identity ascribed in this way is that there is some disincentive to acquire alternative or additional identities, since they can never erase the 'wife of' one.

The nature of the vicarious identity which a wife acquires is not the same as the 'real' occupational identity held by her husband: not only is it a second-hand identity, it also is often second-rate. Eichler has argued that there is a kind of 'shadow' status hierarchy for wives, and if a woman herself works, she will hold a position *both* in this shadow hierarchy, and also be ranked independently on the same criteria as men. The cultural prescription is that a woman's independent status (if any) should be no more than equal to her shadow one (Eichler, 1973, especially pp. 45–7). Writing of the vicarious identity only Acker argues, following Shils, that the degree of deference to which a wife is entitled is usually somewhat less than that offered to the male incumbent of the occupational status: 'Conferred status does not imply equivalent status . . . The recipient of conferred status in most cases probably does not have deference entitlements equivalent to those of the person whose proximity confers deference' (Acker, 1973, p. 492).

These analyses help to fill out the notion of vicarious occupational identities. They are identities conferred upon wives by their husbands' work, and normally form the upper limits of whatever social status is possible for a wife, since it is culturally prescribed that anything which she does in her own right should not have the effect of conferring a status in excess of her husband's. The only culturally approved way in which a wife can improve her social status is through her husband. She is, however, partly compensated for that limitation, by receiving vicarious entitlement to a particular status (and associated privileges) which is probably ranked higher than any she would gain in her own right, because of the cultural assumption that men normally 'marry down' both in terms of status and of age. But this compensation is double-edged: she may acquire certain privileges thereby, but her position is unlikely to be as advantageous as it would be if *she* held the equivalent job.

Drawing Her In: Wives' Contributions to their Husbands' Work

Introduction to Part Two

In the early industrial period, it was not unknown for employers to hire whole familes (Harris, 1969, p. 120; Thompson, 1968, pp. 339–40, 372–4). This practice now survives in formal terms only in a very restricted range of occupations, such as the employment of married couples in residential domestic service, or as house parents in boarding institutions. Indeed, texts on the sociology of the family usually have taken it to be of fundamental importance that the development of an industrial capitalist economy requires the development of a system of wage labour, in which people are employed as individuals (see, for example, discussion of this issue in Harris, 1969, ch. 4). In contemporary Britain an employer normally has no formal, legal obligation to the spouse or children of his or her employees, apart from the important exception of obligations derived from occupational pensions schemes, nor does the employer have any formal right to expect any work from the employee's family.

Whatever the formal, legal position, the reality can be somewhat different. It is not difficult to think of familiar examples where the wife, say, of a diplomat, a politician, or a clergyman becomes identified with that work, to the point of being actively involved in it. These are examples where a wife, to a greater or lesser degree, contributes her own labour in the cause of her husband's work: for example, the well-publicised case of Rosalynn Carter, who supported the work of the President of the United States by having her own office in the White House, making campaign speeches on his behalf and undertaking foreign tours as his representative. After Ronald Reagan's election, journalists were naturally interested to speculate whether his wife would also become 'a major adviser', although she was claiming that she wanted no part in policy decisions (*Guardian*, 3 June 1980, p. 8).

This kind of activity is not confined to the United States: Margaret Lloyd George is said to have 'nursed' her husband's Welsh constituency on his behalf during his prolonged absences in London, and her campaign speeches at election times were important in securing Liberal victories in that part of Wales (McLeod, 1976, pp. 180–207). Such examples as the wives of Presidents and Prime Ministers of course can hardly be regarded as typical; but in terms of what they reveal of assumptions about marriage, and about the relationship of married people to each other's work, they may not be as exceptional as they appear at first. Indeed, it will be argued that such examples are exceptional only in terms of the *opportunities* which they afford for a wife to contribute to her husband's work: the difference between the situation of these women and that of most other wives is a quantitative rather than a qualitative one.

That similar opportunities do exist more widely is reflected in an article in *Family Circle* (a magazine with a wide distribution through supermarkets). This advised wives with successful husbands to learn how to 'back up your man', which apparently is an activity to be practised equally by the full-time housewife and the wife in paid work. 'Show him what a tower of strength a loving and understanding wife can be, whether you are at home with your family or going out to work yourself' (Westland, 1980, p. 86). Advice included: putting his needs and feelings before your own, taking small household concerns off his shoulders, learning to be a good listener, feeding him properly, being efficient at acting as unpaid secretary, and anticipating his travelling needs, like this exemplary wife:

> a friend of mine . . . keeps an overnight bag packed for her husband, complete with spare toilet and shaving gear, night clothes and hair brushes, handkerchiefs and underwear. That only leaves suit, shirts and ties to be laid neatly on top. As a special surprise, she always pops in one of the children's latest drawings or poems – a lovely family touch when he opens his case many miles from home.
>
> (ibid., p. 88)

One can only speculate as to how many men are likely to welcome such surprises, but undoubtedly few would reject the type of treatment recommended. Being relieved of humdrum tasks obviously is very useful, and clearly supports his work.

The chapters in Part Two will explore the ways in which wives commonly contribute to their husbands' work, and some of the processes by which such contributions are elicited. These are grouped under the headings of domestic labour, 'giving moral support' and more direct contributions. As in Part One, the discussion will include some special cases which, although the experience of only a minority, are of particular interest because they highlight some processes of wives' incorporation, and illustrate the extent of incorporation which at least is *possible*.

As before, the emphasis will be upon how particular features of work organisation create particular forms of incorporation. Some features of work organisation which were seen (in Part One) to have very significant structuring effects on wives' lives are much less important for eliciting their contributions. For example, it was argued that shift work in a factory can impose particularly difficult timetables on a wife's life; however, such wives are unlikely to be drawn into their husbands' work in direct ways. On the other hand, some features of work organisation are important on both sides of the coin. Home-based work is one such example: not only does it impose significant structures upon a wife but also, it will be argued, it provides a crucial mechanism through which her contributions can be elicited.

6

Domestic Labour and the Production of the Male Worker

One of the effects of treating work and home as separate spheres, and assuming that productive work takes place only in the former, is to obscure the extent to which household activities, and especially the performance of domestic labour, are economic activities. The recognition that domestic work is indeed an economic activity is being interestingly reflected in the law relating to property allocation on divorce, where increasingly 'the wife's household activity is accounted as one of the forms of contribution of which the law will take cognisance in liquidating matrimonial assets on divorce' (Gray, 1977, p. 67). Domestic labour, however, has significant economic features while the marriage continues, as well as when it ends, and is one of the main ways in which wives contribute to their husbands' work.

Sociological interest in the significance of a woman's domestic labour – both to women themselves, and as a process which maintains particular patterns of social life – has followed the re-emergence of a women's movement. As early as 1966, Hannah Gavron published a small, but subsequently influential, study, which demonstrated the meaning for women themselves of their 'captivity' as domestic wives (Gavron, 1966). A decade later, Ann Oakley produced a much more detailed pair of studies (Oakley, 1974a, 1974b), which documented women's experience of housework, and confirmed that mostly they find it monotonous, fragmented and isolating (Oakley, 1974b, p. 182); the low status of this work serves to confirm and reinforce the low status of these women whose full-time job it is. Alongside this kind of analysis of housework, which focuses upon its meaning and significance for individual women, the so-called 'domestic labour debate' has addressed the issues at a rather different level, examining the contribution of women's domestic labour to the development and maintenance of the industrial-capitalist mode of production. Unlike those analyses which concentrate on women's own experience of housework, the domestic labour debate does locate women's domestic activity in the context of male employment, and does recognise that wives contribute to the maintenance of that structure.

The main issues of this 'debate' have been explored fully elsewhere (Gardiner, 1976; Smith, 1973; Mackintosh, 1979; Rushton, 1979) and will be summarised briefly here, in so far as they relate to the issue of wives' contributions to male employment. Essentially, wives' domestic labour is seen as contributing in a variety of ways to the maintenance of the capitalist mode of production and to 'the reproduction of the conditions of capitalism' (McIntosh, 1979, p. 155). First, through her domestic labour, a wife 'services' the present generation of workers, ensuring that their various physical needs are catered for, thus enabling them to put their full energies into their work, and 'restoring their capacity to endure the next shift' (Secombe, 1974, p. 19). Secondly, a housewife not only oils the wheels of production by servicing the *present* generation of workers, but also she plays a key role in producing the next generation. She nurtures the next generation both by providing physical care, and by reproducing the cultural and ideological conditions which will ensure the continuation of capitalist relations of production. Thus she socialises her children to be the next generation of wage labourers by producing 'young adults who have internalised a repertoire of attitudes and perceptual structures which enable them to self-actualise willingly in an adjusted manner within bourgeois relations' (ibid., p. 15). In both of these activities, a wife effectively provides an economic subsidy, because alternative methods of achieving the same results would be much more costly, whether those costs were borne by male workers, by their employers, or by the state.

From the viewpoint of this study, a key point about domestic labour is that it is performed by women, and in particular, by women *as wives*. The significance of that has usually been overlooked in the domestic labour debate, preoccupied as it has often been by the issue of whether domestic labour under capitalism is value-creating (Rushton, 1979; Smith, 1973). In a very interesting article, Maureen Mackintosh (1979) takes this as her starting-point, and argues that the debate was set up in terms which led into a cul-de-sac precisely because it begged the question of the sexual division of labour within the home: 'the sexual division of labour within the home – that is, the fact that it is women who perform most of the domestic labour – had within the terms of the debate to be taken for granted' (ibid., p. 175). Mackintosh's own way out of this cul-de-sac is to look at domestic labour cross-culturally. This leads her to argue that we need to keep clear analytical distinctions between 'the household' and 'the family' when discussing domestic labour in capitalist societies. This enables one to recognise that the household is an economic institution (producing products for use, for example, cooking, child care), and yet to keep separate the issue of why *marriage* is the basis upon which most households are constituted, and why 'the performance of domestic labour is still closely linked to the status of being a wife' (ibid., p. 189).

There is, in other words, nothing inevitable about the designation of wives as domestic labourers. Even if one can explain a particular form of household production of goods and services as characteristic of, or even functional for, contemporary capitalism, one still has to explain why the relations of production *within* the household entail a particular form of sexual division of labour. In that enterprise, the institution of marriage seems crucial. As Mackintosh puts it, 'the marriage bond is still a subordinating one for women, and domestic labour is the economic content of that subordination' (ibid., p. 189). One needs to look, therefore, at the economic and cultural characteristics of contemporary marriage in order to understand why it is that *wives* are the primary domestic labourers. That issue is addressed at a more general level in Part Three. At this point in the discussion, the important thing to emphasise is that the marriage relationship itself provides the mechanism through which women become domestic labourers, and thus become part of the productive labour undertaken by their husbands.

In what ways does the domestic labour of a wife contribute to her husband's work, and how far can it be seen as making a contribution to capitalist production? The most useful strand in the domestic labour debate at this point is found in those writers who argue that this labour 'produces' the male worker, thus making an important, if apparently indirect, contribution to capitalist production. This essentially is the burden of Secombe's argument when he sees domestic labour as labour which produces *labour power* rather than labour which produces the wage (Secombe, 1974, p. 10).

Although there are problems about developing this argument in the context of a Marxist account of the creation of value (Mackintosh, 1979; Rushton, 1979), the general point can be taken. Wives' domestic labour produces male wage labourers, and capitalist employers benefit thereby. In providing for her husband's well-being, and taking on most (if not all) other domestic tasks, a wife presents her husband's employer with a worker who is fit *for* work, and able to give his undivided attention *to* work. This process is not restricted to particular types of occupation: it is a contribution made by wives of men in *any* type of employment, and it occurs whenever a wife takes on the sole or major responsibility for domestic tasks. Changing customs about husbands 'helping' in the home do not necessarily alter that process.

Leonard has noted that young husbands 'accept that they are competent to do most forms of housework *if necessary*; but they do not *actually do* much cooking, cleaning, washing or tidying' (Leonard, 1980, p. 244) (italics original). Nor is this necessarily altered if a wife herself is in employment. In fact, available evidence on the domestic labour performed by *working* wives tends to suggest that a wife's own employment status is of comparatively little significance for her performance of domestic labour. Men's participation in household tasks increases a little when their wives take paid work, but 'hardly enough to reach parity with their employed wives', especially at the most busy time in the household day, such as early morning (Berk and Berk, 1979, p. 231). The Rapoports' study of working couples also confirms that, even where there is some conscious effort to share housework and child care, and where men take on 'women's tasks', wives continue to take the ultimate responsibility, especially the responsibility for making sure that the work is done by *someone* (Rapoport and Rapoport, 1978, p. 84). As Leonard puts it, 'within marriage, though the division of *tasks* is less rigid . . . the division of *responsibility* is as before' (Leonard, 1980, p. 267).

The particular significance of wives' performance of domestic labour for their husbands' employers is that it enables them to ignore the domestic and child care responsibilities of their male employees or indeed to fail to acknowledge them as responsibilities. They need make no special allowances or arrangements, because they can assume that such responsibilities are being shouldered by wives. Purcell has noted that most jobs in the labour market do not accommodate the timetables set by school hours and pre-school facilities, for example, and assume virtually full-time parental 'cover' in the home (Purcell, 1978, p. 155).

The most dramatic examples of the consequences of employers' ability to ignore the reality that male employees do have children, or infirm dependents, are occupations which entail the employee's absence from home for extended periods of time. Such occupations extend across the whole range of manual, managerial and professional work, and the balance of costs and gains may be somewhat ambiguous from a wife's point of view. It has already been argued (pp. 69–70 above) that work which takes a man away from home for periods of time may be quite auspicious for the wife who wishes to minimise the structuring effects of her husband's work upon her own life. Nevertheless, from the employer's standpoint, being able to assume that wives will 'cover' for domestic responsibilities offers considerable advantages for the management and deployment of the male labour force.

Although men who do this kind of work may argue that their

families derive financial benefits from it (Hollowell, 1968, ch. VI; Young and Willmott, 1973, ch. IX), it is still true that only by virtue of their wives' continuous availability for domestic labour, and total responsibility for child care, can they do these jobs at all. Conversely, wives contribute very significantly to their husbands' employers, by presenting them with employees who are freed from all domestic responsibilities, to undertake work as and when the employer requires. Of course, some couples with higher incomes may employ substitute or supplementary domestic labour, but this does not necessarily negate a wife's contribution: except in unusual cases, she probably will be responsible for supervising the substitute labour. Moreover, the purpose of employing others may precisely be to enable her to support her husband the more, by accompanying him on business trips, for example. However, whatever alternatives are available to the financially favoured, they are by no means the only people who have to spend periods away from home. Any social arrangements which took seriously the fact that men do have children (and also possibly other dependants in need of day-to-day care) would have to come to terms with the need to fund alternative domestic arrangements wherever employees, be they male or female, were required to be absent from home for periods of time. This raises, of course, the whole question of the provision of child care facilities on a day-to-day basis, which is almost always discussed in the context of *women's* employment (Oakley and Oakley, 1979), again illustrating employers' ability to overlook the fact that men also are parents.

So a wife's domestic labour, *inter alia*, frees her husband for work, either by selling his labour or on his own account. Thus, from the perspective of her contributions to her husband's work, the significance of a wife's domestic labour lies not so much in the particular tasks which she performs, but in her assumption of responsibility for whatever 'needs' doing. How that gets defined depends partly on the job he does: just as features of work organisation structure a wife's life, so also do they make possible differing forms of incorporation of a wife's labour in her husband's work.

One 'special case' of this is to be found in literature on the self-employed, where sometimes the performance of domestic labour may be acknowledged quite specifically as aiding the business. Hunt gives an example of a respondent married to a man who runs a mobile grocery business: 'Joyce . . . feels that her domestic labour indirectly assists the family business, although she admits that her husband does not see it that way . . . unless his tea was ready he couldn't go out so quick at night and carry on making money' (Hunt, 1980, p. 48).

Where the husband, whether self-employed or not, works from home, there are increased opportunities for a wife to facilitate his work through domestic labour (Elbert and Glastonbury, 1978, pp. 1–9), as indeed there are increased opportunities for her to make direct contributions (see below, chapter 8). As was demonstrated in Part One, especially in relation to the example of the clergy (pp. 56–7 above), home-based work can have the effect of making a man seem less available to share domestic labour, thus increasing the significance, as well as the extent, of his wife's contribution. This process, however, apparently does not operate symmetrically. Where wives themselves are employed in jobs which are flexible in their work schedule or in their location, rather different processes are at work. Work located in the home is regarded as providing women with an ideal opportunity to be employed while retaining responsibility for domestic work and child care: whether it be professional work, freelance secretarial work, or the 'homeworkers' employed in industrial production. Epstein's study (1971a) of women lawyers in the United States, for example, includes a proportion of women who are in partnership with their husbands. These couples maintained a traditional division of labour in the home, and some had even chosen to live in the immediate vicinity of their work so that the wife (but not the husband) could continue to personally supervise the children.

Apart from rare cases where married couples establish, and succeed in maintaining, a very non-traditional division of labour in the home, the domestic labour of wives represents a very significant mechanism through which employers benefit from the work of people whom they do not employ, and to whom they have almost no legal obligations. The particular significance of this process is that its operation is so widespread in a society like Britain. Although the details of wives' contributions vary with the particular organisation of different occupations, the fact of their contribution does not. Whether the form of their contribution is dictated by their husbands' frequent absence, or by his constant presence, the underlying structure remains: the demands of a man's employment are supreme, and his wife's domestic labour facilitates those demands.

7
Giving Moral Support

The production of an efficient male worker involves his physical production through domestic labour. In many cases, it also involves work on his emotions and other personal needs. This kind of work done by wives essentially is an economic contribution, as is recognised by Gray, writing about the creation of matrimonial property: 'The housewife's domestic activity also has economic significance in the *affectional* domain, in that the emotional gratification provided by her services enables the husband to devote himself more effectively to his role as the family breadwinner' (Gray, 1977, p. 39) (italics original).

This work of the emotional production of the male worker is probably best encapsulated in the notion of giving 'moral support'. Such support can be given both in practical ways – for example, by the way in which domestic work is actually organised – and in interpersonal interactions, that is, the way in which a wife handles her relationship with her husband. Men who do not have wives recognise their disadvantage in this regard. Cardinal Hume was quoted in the press as acknowledging that, whilst he still regarded celibacy as essential for Catholic priests, there are 'times and occasions when it would be marvellous to have a wife'. His further elaboration of the utility of a wife concentrated on emotional support: he would like to have a wife 'to support and to help, and to whom one could talk confidentially and in intimacy about what was a worry, what was an anxiety and what was burdening' (*Guardian*, 3 February 1981).

Whilst specific opportunties for giving moral support obviously vary somewhat in different jobs, the 'need' for some degree of support is commonly said to be generated in men just by their participation in the public domain. The domestic domain is designated as the place where such needs should be met, even if it cannot do so very effectively. Thus argues Lasch, in a passage where the use of the male form is significant, but appears unintentionally so: 'As business, politics and diplomacy grow more savage and warlike, men seek a haven in private life, in personal relations, and above all in the family – the last refuge of love and decency. Domestic life, however, seems increasingly incapable of providing these comforts' (Lasch, 1977, p. i).

Since one common theme is that the 'needs' generated in male workers include needs for comfort, warmth and an undemanding environment (Comer, 1974, pp. 237–44), one obvious way in which a wife can give personal support is by the way she performs domestic labour, organising the home so that it places minimal demands upon her worker-husband and provides a comfortable environment in which he can relax. A wife, as Lopata puts it, is 'the person responsible for converting the "house into a home" by manipulating its form' (Lopata, 1971, p. 181).

The wives of men in very different kinds of work give this as a rationale for their activities as housewives. In their study of a mining community, where work and home were completely separate worlds, Dennis, Henriques and Slaughter (1969) showed that an integral part of the mining culture was the belief that wives had the responsibility of organising the home so as to make as few demands as possible upon men. It was very important for the home to be 'a haven for the tired man when he returns from work; here he expects to find a meal prepared, a room clean and tidy, a seat comfortable and warm, and a wife ready to give him what he wants – in fact the very opposite of the place to has just left, with its noise, dirt, darkness, toil, impersonalism and no little discomfort' (ibid., p. 179). In a completely contrasting working situation, similar sentiments can be found: wives of the clergy also see themselves as having a duty to provide a trouble-free, demand-free domestic environment. The great majority of them give strong assent to the view that 'The first duty of a clergyman's wife is to her home and family', and it is common to hear views such as

> My job is being Bill's wife, and keeping the home running smoothly so that he can do his job better.   (Spedding, 1975, pp. 295–6)

But domestic labour is only one means by which wives attempt to cater for their husbands' work-generated needs. Often a wife tries to meet those needs at the interpersonal level, by the way she treats her husband and speaks to him. Sometimes this may involve *refraining* from certain actions or words: at the very least, a wife must not rock the boat. For example, a manager's wife apparently may facilitate her husband's work 'by *not* complaining when her husband works late; by *not* fussing when a transfer is coming up; by *not* engaging in any controversial activity' (Whyte, 1971, p. 80).

Sometimes the 'moral support' given to a husband can benefit his work fairly directly. The Pahls report that some managers' wives act as 'sounding boards' for their husbands or that their relationship with their wives gives them confidence in business (Pahl and Pahl, 1971, p. 95), and the same apparently can be true of doctors' wives (Fowlkes, 1980, p. 108). This is supported by another study of managing directors, where one appreciated the value of a wife who was 'someone of great ability with whom he could discuss his business problems in confidence' (Young and Willmott, 1973, p. 259).

Thus, through the mechanism of giving moral support, and by meeting needs created in work, wives can be seen to be contributing to their husbands' work in ways which are both direct and indirect. They contribute indirectly by creating a supportive home environment, which contrasts with work, and restores the male worker to his full capacity. As Comer puts it in her analysis of marriage, 'A wife and home siphon off the discontents which, if left untreated, would endanger his continued exploitation at work and threaten the very foundations of the production process' (Comer, 1974, pp. 237–8). Some also contribute more directly, by offering a relationship through which their husband can work through problems and strategies which will enable him to do his job more effectively. This is not to suggest that all wives give this support uniformly, or that all marriage relationships are equally supportive in this sense; but that in so far as a wife *does* provide this support, her husband's work, and consequently his employer, can be seen to be reaping the benefits.

How far should these activities be regarded simply as optional extras for a wife? The answer depends partly on how far she adheres to, or feels able to break away from, the 'helpmeet' model. Although some would argue that the images of the 'contented helpmeet in the happy home and the tired warrior in the jungle outside' were blurring even in the 1960s (Rapoport and Rapoport, 1976, p. 345), there seems ample reason for regarding them as by no means extinguished. It seems that most married women are still drawn into the helpmeet role, especially where a husband's job is one which is prestigious and important, and where it has particular moral worth attached to it. So, as a man rises through the status hierarchy of an organisation, it becomes increasingly difficult for his wife to fail to act as a helpmeet (Mortimer, Hall and Hill, 1978, p. 291). In explaining why so few directors' wives had a paid job in comparison with wives of other men, Young and Willmott suggest that, not simply are they financially more comfortable, but also they feel that they could not be adequate directors' wives if they did work (Young and Willmott, 1973, pp. 252–5).

The obligation to be a helpmeet perhaps is felt most strongly where one's husband's job is one of public importance, or highly valued for some other reasons. The tendency for wives to become most closely identified with their husband's work when that work is highly prestigious or socially valued has been attributed to the worker's own increased commitment to his work. 'A greater sense of importance may generate higher individual commitment to work, and greater interest and support on the part of his wife and other family members'

(Mortimer, Hall and Hill, 1978, p. 295). This kind of moral imperative, to support a man who is doing a highly valued job, is felt also by wives of the clergy, although they have neither the financial compensations of directors' wives nor the reflected prestige of wives of diplomats or statesmen. Nevertheless, since overwhelmingly they are practising Christians themselves, they place high value on their husbands' work, and feel not only obliged, but also privileged, to spend a good deal of time and energy in supporting him (Finch, 1980).

The force of the moral imperative to be a helpmeet derives not simply from traditional cultural prescriptions for a wife, but is reinforced by employers who *expect* that wives will provide this kind of support. This is particularly the case, again, where men are potential candidates for promotion, for positions of key responsibility, or for public office: Gowler and Legge note that 'Organisations tend to assume that wives of their career committed employees will provide a flexible and supportive domestic environment' (Gowler and Legge, 1978, p. 51). Sometimes employers may take steps to try to ensure that their key employees *do* have supportive wives, as when informal vetting takes place (see above, p. 64). Such procedures are indicative of the extent to which the structure of employment is predicated on the assumption that men, at the very least 'important' men, will be backed by a supportive wife. The interests of employers, requiring a morally bolstered (as well as physically healthy) work-force, coincide neatly with the traditional expectations of a wife: together they produce strong pressure for a wife to be a 'helpmeet', especially if her husband does work which is commonly regarded as socially important or useful. Thus a job which imposes special kinds of constraints upon a wife because it is vicariously contaminating (see above, pp. 37–42) also is significant for the ways in which she is likely to be drawn into it.

8

Two for the Price of One: Peripheral Activities

Discussion so far has centred on wives' contributions which broadly are indirect contributions, in that they are made through the male worker, mostly having the effect of facilitating his work performance. Although indirect, they are by no means insignificant, if only because they are so widespread: they represent the means by which large numbers of wives support the work of male employees, and their employers.

Beyond these, opportunities do exist for a wife sometimes to participate actively in aspects of her husband's work, thus making a direct contribution through her own labour but for no additional financial reward. As in Part One, it will be argued that features of the organisation of men's work are of particular significance, in that they create different *forms* in which a wife's labour is incorporated in her husband's work. Features of work which seem especially important for drawing wives directly in are: home-based work, work which entails being a 'public figure', work where it is possible for a wife to accompany her husband for part of the time, work which involves a number of tasks which look like 'women's work', and work which is greatly facilitated if someone can always be contacted in the worker's absence.

The discussion of wives' direct contributions has been divided into three linked ways in which employers get two for the price of one: peripheral activities and (in the following two chapters) back-up services and the additional worker.

The businessman's wife who entertains his clients, or the MP's wife who gets to know a constituency well by living there, is engaging in an activity which, although peripheral in the sense of not being central to the day-to-day demands of her husband's work, nevertheless can be important to the smooth conduct of his work, and ultimately for his success. The importance of having a wife who will do this is obviously recognised by politicians, and indeed may be one of the mechanisms by which able women get their own potential careers de-railed (Papanek, 1973, p. 852). Margaret Jackson, former minister in the DES, has described how, before she became an MP, her talent was recognised by Fred Peart (for whom she worked) who suggested that the appropriate future for her was as the supportive wife of a male politician:

> He kept saying how marvellous I was. One day he said, 'I can't think why you don't settle down and marry some nice young Labour M.P. It would be such a help to his career'. I said it was very nice of him, but actually I would rather have the career myself. He looked totally thrown. (*Guardian*, 13 May 1980, p. 8)

Peripheral activities can entail a wife's being a channel of information *from* the clientele *to* her husband; conversely, she can act as her husband's advocate or representative *to* his clientele, actual or potential. Such activities may indeed be extended, as Pahl has suggested, to the informal economy: 'it may be that one member of the household provides the tradeable skill and the other markets it through a social network. A wife may publicise her husband's ability to tune cars or a husband may find clients for his wife's skills as a dressmaker' (Pahl, R. E., 1980, p. 7).

In the sphere of paid employment, academic research provides a good example of the potential for wives' peripheral contributions. Platt, in her study of social researchers, quotes the following examples of wives' assistance for husbands doing participant observation and similar studies:

> a very attractive wife smoothed relationships with key informants . . . another wife acquired relevant information through her job. One teacher wife provided useful background data for her husband's research by setting appropriate essay topics for the children she taught to write on. A girlfriend of appropriate background proved useful in another project as a deliberately planted observer on the local organisation of a political party to which the researchers were known not to be sympathetic. (Platt, 1976, pp. 122–3)

This kind of help, although clearly a significant contribution to the work, was almost always unpaid, and Platt notes that she could find only two cases where husbands gave equivalent assistance with their wives' research.

Doctors' wives, in the United States at least, have many opportunities to support their husbands' work by engaging in community activities, since the doctor's wife is 'expected to display her support for her husband's service to the community . . . in ways which will reflect back on the seriousness and centrality of his work commitment; her identity becomes an extension of his and as his adjunct she proclaims his good work through her own' (Fowlkes, 1980, p. 46). Such activities, involving primarily volunteer work and associated social activities, have been institutionalised for American doctors' wives around organisations such as the Women's Auxiliary of the American Medical Association (ibid., pp. 46–9).

Other examples of wives' peripheral contributions taking on institutional forms can be found, not surprisingly, where wives live in institutional settings. One such example can be found in the military services, where the tradition that officers' wives take on the 'welfare' visiting of the wives of other ranks remains strong, despite many wives' dislike of it. The report on army welfare found that over half the wives of senior officers liked 'calling on soldiers' wives to see how they are' (Ministry of Defence, 1976, Table 15), but less than 27 per cent overall of junior officers' wives liked visiting (ibid., para. 281). This apparently increased ambivalence about visiting is reflected in written documents. Two examples illustrate this well. The first is from a letter to the *SAAFA Magazine* in 1967, expressing the view that visiting is an automatic part of being an officer's wife, and describing it as a 'job':

> The average army officer's wife has been brought up from subaltern days to accept visiting as part of her job. It is the very least we can do to help these wives of men who are, after all, our husbands' responsibility.   (*SAAFA Magazine*, April 1967, p. 7)

A decade later, the army welfare inquiry report apparently wished to encourage the view that visiting is optional:

> [Visiting] should be undertaken voluntarily by those who have the time and talent to play a friendly and supportive role to soldiers' wives and families. It follows that those who are not able to accept a welfare role are in *no sense failing to reach the standards expected of them*. (Ministry of Defence, 1976, para. 282) (my italics)

The implication here is that visiting is optional in the sense that negative sanctions should not be applied to those who do not do it. However, that in no way undermines the potential rewards which may accrue to those who do. Indeed, one may speculate that where such an activity is officially regarded as 'voluntary', those who *do* visit have, if anything, enhanced potential for supporting and promoting their husbands' work.

In rather less rigid institutional settings, probably the most obvious example of peripheral activities is wives' entertaining of clients and colleagues, although it may be possible to overestimate the numerical significance of the 'business' entertaining. The wives of middle managers, according to the Pahls, found that entertaining and being entertained in connection with their husbands' work formed a relatively small part of their lives (Pahl and Pahl, 1971, p. 193). Fowlkes reported that the wives of academics in her study felt that entertaining within the faculty had diminished considerably in recent years (Fowlkes, 1980, pp. 64–5).

The opportunities for entertaining probably vary in different settings. For example, Baker's study suggests a high level of business entertaining when American company wives are overseas (Baker, 1976, p. 347). Although there is no comparative data in this study, it seems possible that being in a foreign country as a businessman's wife may provide both increased opportunity and additional rationales for entertaining. Even in other settings, it would be wrong to assume that business entertaining has necessarily diminished, despite its sometimes being regarded as rather 'traditional'. Particular benefits may derive from entertaining where the husband owns the business himself. Preliminary evidence from Deem's study of women and leisure in Milton Keynes shows that wives of men with small businesses do still get involved in entertaining. 'Women with husbands or partners involved in running businesses found that they had to spend time visiting business colleagues, attending social functions and entertaining business acquaintances, which they might otherwise have spent on their own leisure' (Deem, 1981, p. 7). Similarly Scase and Goffee, in their study of small businesses, found that, as the business expanded, wives were more likely to become involved in entertaining potential customers, maintaining company 'morale' and participating in local organisations. This they see as the wife 'representing the family and the company symbolically' (Scase and Goffee, 1980b, p. 221).

The *frequency* with which this happens perhaps is not so important as the fact that the *opportunity* still exists for a wife to further her husband's career by appropriate involvement in entertaining. Sometimes this may involve simply accompanying her husband to a restaurant while he entertains clients: apparently her very presence can be good for business. According to one of Young and Willmott's sample of managing directors,

> If a man wants you to go out to dinner and you haven't got your wife, he has to leave his wife out. If your wife is there, his wife can come too. Often wives get to know each other, and it's good for them *and* good for business. (Young and Willmott, 1973, p. 260)

Entertainment and the provision of hospitality certainly are not the exclusive prerogative of managers' wives. On the one hand, wives of the clergy report that they provide endless cups of tea for their husbands' clients; and, on a very different scale, diplomats' wives in foreign postings become involved in a whole lifestyle of entertaining and being entertained. In her article on diplomats' wives, Callan makes clear the obligatory nature of the former: the internal literature of the diplomatic service stresses 'the importance of a wife's role and says, for example, that her attendance at parties (especially those of the Head of Mission) is, except in cases of domestic emergency, compulsory' (Callan, 1975, pp. 94–5). The task of 'official' entertaining, which is part of the work of all senior diplomats, is one which will, it is assumed, be shared by the wife: on occasions, it is assumed that the wife will take the major part of the burden of this (ibid., p. 95). In undertaking these tasks, a wife not only contributes her domestic labour and managerial skills, but also is required to stage a performance which demonstrates a fair degree of quite specialised social and political skills, which she is presumed to possess by virtue of being married to a diplomat. Such skills can be very useful indeed to her husband's employer. When Lord Soames was appointed Governor General of Rhodesia and given the task of negotiating arrangements for that country's independence, press speculation included the observation that 'it is not unlikely that the decision to send Lord Soames was influenced by the fact that Mary Soames' warm and open personality would be a major asset during their stay in Government House' (*Guardian*, 12 December 1979, p. 11). Such talents are not merely a bonus for the diplomatic service, but in a sense are *expected* of wives. Callan suggests that 'for some purpose, wives can be presumed to have capacities commensurate with their husband's rank', and quotes the telling remark, 'If you were a security guard's wife, we wouldn't expect you to show political judgement' (ibid., footnote 9, p. 103). Although it is assumed *that* a wife will possess such skills, as appropriate to her husband's rank, it is not at all clear *how* to acquire them, other than by assimilation over the breakfast table, presumably.

The assumption that wives will possess certain skills useful in their husbands' work often is related to their presumed activities as wives and mothers. Thus diplomats' wives are useful as good hostesses – as an extension of their presumed wifely activities – and doctors' wives are thought of as good receptionists because they will be suitably warm and motherly. That was the view of one contributor to a House of Lords debate about proposed legislation which would allow a doctor's wife to be paid for services performed as receptionist for her husband: 'The wives can give comfort, help and assurance which often a receptionist – no matter how qualified she may be – may not have the skills to do. She may not be as mature as the wife who may have a family of her own' (parliamentary Debates, House of Lords, Vol. 411, col. 1378, 10 July 1980).

To some extent the onus presumably is upon men to select wives who will be able and willing to perform appropriately, and there is a sense in which such performances are very specifically part of being a *middle class* wife. Gillespie characterises this as 'The middle-class wife must be understanding and helpful when [her husband] has problems at work and must do a good job of representing him socially to his work associates, the boss and clients when that is necessary' (Gillespie, 1972, p. 132). From a wife's point of view, the situation is structured so as to encourage, even to oblige, her acquiescence. Although the example of diplomatic entertaining undoubtedly is rather special, it is a good illustration of a point which is more generally applicable: in certain occupations, there exists the real possibility that a wife's actions or words can inflct serious damage upon her husband's present work, and his future career prospects. The effects of that implied sanction are twofold: it may provide a stimulus to competent performance, but by the same token it acts as a powerful constraint against any refusal to fit the mould. The spectre of the clergyman's wife who 'refused to have anything to do with the church and ruined her husband's ministry' is one conjured up by many clergy wives, even though they interpret their own conforming performance as a willing contribution, rather than as a result of fearing the consequences of non-participation (Spedding, 1975, pp. 256–7). Nevertheless, the existence of such a powerful sanction forms part of the process through which wives' contributions are elicited, especially in those occupations where *her* 'failure' is interpreted as reflecting badly upon her husband. Where a wife herself places high value upon her husband's work, this sanction will be all the more powerful.

9

Two for the Price of One: Back-Up Services

Although the boundaries between 'peripheral' and 'back-up' services cannot be drawn neatly, the category of 'back-up services' is used here to denote those activities which, unlike those in the 'peripheral' category, are central to the daily performance of a man's work, but of a routine and non-specialised character. Fowlkes characterises these as 'girl Friday' contributions, which she sees mainly as providing semi-skilled 'women's work' services (Fowlkes, 1980, pp. 64–5).

The possibilities for this kind of contribution vary with different types of work: as appropriate, a wife (and indeed other members of the family) may find herself answering the telephone, taking messages, filing, or dealing with visits from clients or sales representatives. Some wives may be doing this on a regular basis, and others become incorporated just at times of crisis, or when their husbands' work load is particularly heavy; for example, when a report has to be written to meet a deadline, or in a pre-election period. Platt reports that wives of social researchers were incorporated, usually unpaid, 'to help with typing, routine statistical tests, or hand counting of data when a computer is not available' (Platt, 1976, p. 123). Similarly, a study of East Anglian farmers reports that about three-quarters of farmers' wives were providing services such as 'answering the phone, dealing with callers, and running the occasional farm errand' (Newby, Bell, Rose and Saunders, 1978, p. 68). It may well be that this figure of three-quarters actually under-represents the participation of farmers' wives across the whole spectrum of farming. Certainly the traditional pattern of hill farms was that wives and daughters provided almost all the female labour (Williams, 1969, pp. 33 ff).

The use of the home as a workbase is, again, one type of work organisation likely to draw a wife into providing back-up services. If a self-employed man, for example, does not have the facilities of a separate office, the home is likely to become the focus both for requests for his services and for the administration of his work, and ample scope is provided for a wife's incorporation. This would apply to a self-employed journalist, driving instructor, window-cleaner, or a whole range of high and low status jobs. Even where the husband is an employee, the use of the home is likely to draw in his wife. This is well illustrated by Cain's work on the police, where the wife of the rural policeman (whose home is also a police station) 'is expected, if not formally required, to take telephone messages and attend to callers in her husband's absence' (Cain, 1973, p. 127). Exactly the same applies to wives of the clergy, who all, without exception, reported their involvement in this kind of work.

A wife's availability for these routine back-up tasks is related in part to her own employment status; but certainly for full-time housewives such apparently trivial activities represent a not inconsiderable contribution to their husbands' work. In terms of time taken up, it can be experienced as a significant commitment: certainly, some wives of the clergy experience it as a constant demand (Spedding, 1975, ch. 9, sect. d). Material from my study of clergymen's wives provides a good illustration of how living 'over the shop', as it were, creates the setting for drawing a wife into activities connected with her husbands' work. The following diary extract represents a very ordinary day for this respondent:

Day: Wednesday
   Got up at: 8.20

Morning:
   8.20 to 9.30   Letters, breakfast
   9.30 to 11.30   Lady help arrived and we washed table linen and tea towels. Cleared chairs and tables away after a party the previous day for one of our oldest Mother's Union members 90th birthday.
   11.00 to 1.00   Put up new washing line. Started lunch. Made cup of tea. Made bed. Shopping. Take in washing and iron part of it.
   Lunch at: 1.00

Afternoon:
   1.30 to 2.30   Rest and listen to radio.
   2.30 to 3.30   Finish ironing. Start repairs on table cloths for new hall.
   3.30 to 4.50   Made cup of tea for husband (returned from visiting) and church cleaner. Open church up again to receive three trestle tables lent for a 21st party.

                              10 minutes spent clearing up papers and rubbish
                              blown into the garden.
Evening meal at: 4.50.

Evening:
  5.45 to 7.00   Open Church up for Girls Friendly Society.
                              Children in and out of the vicarage for toilet,
                              borrow pens, wash hands, etc. Leader of Girls
                              Brigade picks up subs tin and correspondence
                              case, and goes off to local school. A quick cup of
                              tea.
  7.00 to 7.15   6 children come for a meeting about a holiday in
                              Snowdonia.
  7.15 to 10.00   Let Sunday School teachers into study for a lesson.
                              Wash up. Watch T.V. Have a word with Brigade
                              leader returning case.
Went to bed at: 11.30

                                                    (Spedding, 1975, pp. 279–80)

This respondent was involved throughout the day essentially in trivial
aspects of the organisation of church affairs, and most of these arose
from the fact that she was 'on the spot': if the church or hall needed to
be opened up, she did it, when the church cleaner needed a cup of tea,
she provided it, and when a children's group was meeting in the hall,
she was on hand to provide for their needs.

Such back-up services, whilst apparently trivial in their content,
make a crucial difference to the effectiveness of a man's work, and
often can *only* be provided by a wife, as the person always on the spot.
Precisely the same would be true of the wives of doctors who run GP
practices from their homes. In her opening speech in the House of
Lords debate on the issue of allowing doctors' wives to be paid for this
kind of work, Lady Masham quoted a letter from a GP which
demonstrates that the services he requires can only be provided by a
wife:

The obvious step would be for my wife to resign as secretary-
receptionist, but [it would be] simply impossible to find anyone to
take her place. For the appointment system to work effectively the
telephone is in almost constant use from 8 a.m. to midday and again
from 4 p.m. to 8 p.m. (Parliamentary Debates, House of Lords, Vol.
411, col. 1376, 10 July 1980)

It is interesting to note that these services provided by doctors' wives
were at least being acknowledged as work, and thus deserving of

remuneration, although equivalent work performed by other wives is not always so recognised. It may perhaps be that the greater use of group practice makes it apparent that the work is done *for the practice* rather than simply *for the husband*, thus removing one of the key processes which makes non-payment for this work seem quite natural (see below, pp. 153–7).

Although time spent should not be discounted, perhaps the significance of this type of contribution is not so much its quantity as its consistency and reliability. As Lady Masham put it in the same debate, 'When a doctor is on call, so is his wife. If he is out on call and someone telephones or calls with an emergency it is the wife who in most cases has to take the message or deal with the patient' (ibid.). In this way, wives are very much doing the job of the secretary who holds the fort while the boss is out of the office. However, in providing this kind of front-line service, wives (like secretaries) may well become involved in decisions *about* their husbands' work: should a caller be referred to another agency, is a telephone call urgent enough to call her husband out of a meeting, and so on. Thus, not only is the service offered improved by a wife's participation, but also the path is smoothed for her husband by the operation of a filtering mechanism, so that, for example, certain queries never reach him. Sometimes the filtering may involve diverting the query to another agency; at other times a wife may simply do the job herself. Clergy wives, for example, report that they often open up the church, gives out Banns Forms, or take a booking for the church hall, if this kind of request is made when their husband is not at home (Spedding, 1975, ch. 9, sect. d).

This discussion of back-up services has concentrated mainly on examples of work based in the home, and this serves to emphasise the significance of home-based work in creating a special form of wives' incorporation. The fact that a wife is on the spot (and she will be there at least for part of the time, even if she goes out to work herself), not simply makes her a rather obvious source of help, but also changes the character of decisions about participating in her husband's work. Probably very few wives would take a decision to go out to their husbands' office and act as unpaid secretary there; but when one *lives* in one's husband's office, the question becomes much more one of how to *avoid* involvement, rather than whether to seek it. If the wife of a home-based worker were to avoid contributing to his work, presumably she would have to refuse to answer the telephone or take messages, and claim total ignorance of any aspect of her husband's work. A similar situation occurs where work is 'brought home' from an outside office or other work location. The typist-wife of an academic, for example, may not go to his office to help out, but it is much less easy

for her to sit and watch television while he pounds away with two
fingers, trying to meet the deadline for an article. In this case also, the
presence of the work activity within the home changes the character of
a wife's decision about participating in it. In fact, radical avoidance
strategies would be necessary if a wife wanted to remain uninvolved
(Finch, 1980, p. 868). However, given the economic and cultural
pressures for wives in general to be supportive of their husbands' work
(see below, chapter 12), it seems likely that home-based work creates a
situation in which that support is almost inevitably expressed by a
wife's being drawn into the work itself.

10
Two for the Price of One: the Additional Worker

'Back-up' services, it has been suggested, can shade into activities which amount to making decisions about one's husband's job, or actually doing some of it for him. This chapter concentrates upon those situations where wives do actually take part in their husbands' work. Again, the possibilities for this are enhanced where work is located at home, and also are related to the character of the job, and the skills which a wife can offer. Examples of wives acting as unpaid assistants will be divided broadly into three types: instances where a wife works *instead of* her husband, where she works '*by proxy*' and where she works *alongside* him.

The possibility of a wife's working *instead of* her husband usually occurs in his absence, often in a crisis, and clearly is related to her own range of competence and the type of work involved. Unless medically qualified herself, a doctor's wife will not prescribe drugs or give complex treatments; however, the rural GP's wife may well find herself giving minor treatments, or advice about whether a particular condition requires urgent attention, whether or not she has any medical or related qualification. There is a sense in which simply being married to a doctor is presumed to give her some kind of competence, which she acquires presumably, as the diplomat's wife acquires political skills, over the breakfast table. The same applies to other wives; Cain shows how the wives of rural policemen will take minor 'policing' action in the absence of their husband, including in the following case, which was acknowledged to be rather extreme: 'One wife took upon herself the task of dealing with an accident single-handed, this being by its nature . . . a task requiring a considerable amount of organisation of witnesses and public services, as well as attention to any injured parties' (Cain, 1973, p. 128). Working instead of one's husband does not only occur in his absence. Fowlkes gives an example of an academic's wife, herself a Ph.D., who reads and summarises articles for her husband, and marks students' essays (Fowlkes, 1980, pp. 71–2).

Apart from providing a very clear case of the employer getting two for the price of one, this kind of example also demonstrates the comparative disadvantage of not having a wife. All women, and non-married men, who have to compete on career ladders with married men will find themselves potentially competing with the resources made available by having access to an additional worker, who can be drawn in if necessary.

A second category of examples where wives act as unpaid assistants can be termed 'by proxy' activities; that is, a wife undertakes an activity, not because simply her husband is unavailable or too busy and she is stepping in as second-best, but *because* she is his wife, acting in some sense 'in her own right'. These 'by proxy' situations arise most commonly where the man is in a 'public figure' job, and sometimes there may be a formal and recognised position for the wife. In the diplomatic service, for example, foreign missions have at least two completely formalised wives' positions: the Ambassadress and the Doyenne, the wife of the Ambassador, and of the Dean of the Diplomatic Corps. In each of these cases, the woman concerned has formal duties laid upon her (Callan, 1975, p. 93). Wives of politicians, both local and national, are another example; and again some political offices have an institutionalised consort position (such as lady mayoress) which is usually, but not exclusively, filled by the wife of the incumbent. These institutionalised consort roles are very obvious and visible examples, and perhaps therefore are less significant for understanding the process of wives' incorporation just *because* they are institutionalised: the duties are fairly explicit, expenses are available for undertaking them and it has long been established that they can be undertaken by someone other than a wife. However, normally they are filled by someone else only where there is no wife: a wife's *refusal* to take on such a role would be something quite different, and indicates the strength of the expectation that this is a desirable activity for a wife.

Although these are the most obvious examples, 'by proxy' contributions occur in other settings: wives can do 'by proxy' work even when it is not required by a formalised consort role, or when they move *beyond* what the role requires of them. Thus Rosalynn Carter did not simply act as the gracious hostess in the White House, but had her own office there; indeed, in recent years the President's mother and son, as well as his wife, have undertaken representational duties abroad. At the British royal wedding in 1981, the presidents of Uganda, Ghana and Zambia were represented by their wives; and

Nancy Reagan represented not only the United States President but (along with the Prime Minister of Turkey) the NATO heads of state (*Guardian*, 25 July 1981).

So it appears that where a deputy has to be found for a President it is quite appropriate to send his wife, rather than, for example, a government minister, although she has not stood for any office, nor been appointed to one. In similarly exhalted circles, Margaret Jay has described how she deputised for her husband when he was British ambassador in Washington:

> People want him to speak all over the country, go to various functions, and he literally can't do it all. So what we've done – and it seems to work quite well so far – where it seems to be appropriate, Peter would write back and say: Look I'm awfully sorry, this time I can't make it. Would you like Margaret to come? And actually, people have responded very warmly, they've said, yes please.
>
> (Jay, 1977)

Not only is Margaret Jay acting as an additional, unpaid worker, but she regards her acceptance as a progressive move:

> It's quite nice to think that attitudes have changed sufficiently that when, for example, a foreign affairs club in Chicago asks the British ambassador to come and talk to them, they are prepared to accept that his wife is sufficiently capable to take up the role if he can't do it.
>
> (ibid.)

This last point underlines the significance of 'by proxy' activities; they are underpinned by a presumed competence and expertise on the part of a wife. This may be related partly to her actual experience and skills, but these in themselves do not legitimate her activities: it is her position as 'wife of' which provides the legitimation, and enables her to do this type of work. It is work which could not be undertaken except from the position of wife, and that position gives it authority and acceptability, although the wife who does it is neither formally appointed nor paid.

The third category of wives working as unpaid assistants are those who work *with* their husband, in the sense of alongside him, and under his direction. This is possible only in a limited range of occupations, although that range is increased where the wife herself has some competence in the same field. For example, it might not be normal for an accountant's wife to help him balance the books, but where she too is a qualified accountant, that would be a possibility. Such examples may not necessarily be rare, especially in certain professional groups. Academics are one group whose wives may well have a certain amount of expertise in relevant fields, at least extending to the ability to read critically, and comment upon, work in progress. In the American context, Helen Hughes has demonstrated both the expertise of American faculty wives and their difficulties in obtaining employment in their own right (Hughes, 1973). Fowlkes's study confirms that wives of academics often have similar backgrounds to their husbands', and indeed that their occupational status at the time of marriage was often not too different from his. Doctors' wives, however, whilst they had often worked in medical settings, had usually been doing traditionally female, low status work before their marriage (Fowlkes, 1980, pp. 37–40).

The possibility of a wife's alongside her husband does not always depend upon her prior knowledge or expertise. Wives of the clergy have often had the 'unpaid curate' label attached to them; and, whilst on the whole they reject this as *pre*scription, as *de*scription it is not wildly inaccurate. Many of them implicitly (and sometimes explicitly) regard their husband's church as 'our' church, see their own role very much in 'helpmeet' terms, and work alongside their husbands by being very active in (and perhaps taking total responsibility for) the 'women's work' of the church – women's organisations, children's organisations, and the quasi-domestic tasks associated with church activities (Spedding, 1975, ch. 9). Policemen's wives, especially those who work in country areas where their home is also the police station, become involved in similar ways. Thirty-four per cent of the police wives in Mitchell's study said that they played an active part in police work (Mitchell, 1975, p. 84). As with clergy wives, policemen's wives often do 'women's work' associated with police work. One of Cain's (1973) respondents, a rural police wife, described how it was 'her job' to provide meals for prisoners in the police station cells:

One Saturday, the inspector told my husband, yes [the prisoners] were sure to be away before lunch. Well, Derek didn't go until eleven o'clock on Saturday morning, and then the inspector said that they would be here for lunch after all. Well, he came rushing back and told me about quarter to one. Well, you know how it is when you cook for four, there isn't any to spare, not with the price things are these days. Well, as it happens, I'd got some sausages in the fridge, and we managed to find them some cauliflower and vegetables. Of course, they give you 2/6d. a meal, so you're not out of pocket. It covers your costs, and it's part of my job here.

(Cain, unpublished data)

Particular opportunities for acting as an additional worker are afforded to wives of men who run small businesses, shops, or public houses, and they often regard themselves as a 'team', running a joint enterprise. In these circumstances, the economic contribution made by a wife is often especially apparent. The study of small shopkeepers by Bechhofer *et al.* provides an example here. They write: 'where the small trader *must* call upon resources other than his own, he is forced to involve his family in the affairs of the shop. The small shop frequently is a family shop. Many a marginal enterprise is kept afloat only by the concerted efforts of the husband, wife and children' (Bechhofer, Elliot, Rushforth and Bland, 1974b, p. 479). Such observations are common in most studies of the self-employed. Kohl notes that the family farm in north America 'depends on the labour of its household members' (Kohl, 1977, p. 47); and Stacey's earlier study of Banbury showed that, where there is a family business or shop, 'fathers and sons or brothers work together and mothers take phone calls and help with the office work' (Stacey, 1960, p. 137).

Stacey's perceptive observation about sexual divisions in the family enterprise is also illustrated by a number of other studies. Again, wives are often assigned 'women's work', especially office work, associated with the business. One of Festing's respondents, a fisherman's wife, observed that 'I also do the books; I think you'll find that most of the females do' (Festing, 1977, p. 157). The economic significance of such contributions is well illustrated by one of Scase and Goffee's respondents, a small business owner:

My wife does all the wages on a Thursday night and the end of the month accounts. She looks at the mail in the mornings and shoves the invoices in the envelopes. She also answers the phone and keeps people away from me, if you know what I mean. *If I didn't have her, I would have to employ somebody who would cost me at least £3,500.* This is one of the perks of the business in that *I can show my wife as earning so much money on the books but in fact she doesn't draw any* – it's still kept in the business.
(Scase and Goffee, 1980b, p. 220 (my italics)

The input of this wife's labour clearly is of material significance for the success of the business, although she receives no direct financial rewards. Even more vital to the success of the business, apparently, are the wives of independent bakers in France. Because the wife customarily acts as shopkeeper, she will be the one who promotes or discourages custom: 'the key role is played not by the baker but by his wife. In the competition between small bakeries, the appeal of the baker's wife plays a greater role than the quality of the bread, which does not vary much from one shop to the other. Small shops have a personality of their own, and customers choose them (or abandon them) according to this' (Bertaux and Bertaux-Wiame, 1981, p. 163).

Examples of small businesses are, in one way, quite untypical, since a wife is not gratuitously giving her labour to her husband's *employer* but into 'the business', which she presumably perceives as 'our' business. Often this is expressed in the metaphor of a 'team', running a joint enterprise. That notion of 'team', whilst having at least a superficial relevance to the self-employed, can wear rather thin even for them. Kohl reports that, on family farms, if wives do start to behave as if they actually were a partner in the enterprise, business contacts may decline to take them seriously. It is a 'common experience of women who attempt to transact business for the enterprise, [to be] fobbed off with explanations implying that the agent would prefer to talk to the husband, in order to obtain an authoritative response' (Kohl, 1977, p. 51).

Outside the structure of self-employment, it makes even less sense to see the employed man and his incorporated wife as a 'team', but that is precisely the model which many wives both endorse and welcome. Clergy wives present it as a very positive aspect of their own situation: wives of men newly entering the ministry commonly anticipated their new lifestyle as 'working as a partnership', and more experienced clergy wives valued this opportunity not only for the work itself, but as an aspect of 'sharing', which they saw as central to the marriage relationship. As one said,

> I feel, as a wife, you've got to support your husband, very much so. If you're going to share everything, as you do in marriage – marriage is a matter of sharing things. If John didn't share his work with me, I wouldn't feel it was right, I wouldn't feel we were complete . . . I don't see how you couldn't become involved if you were complete in your marriage.   (Spedding, 1975, p. 256)

The 'team' image obviously has great attractions but the implied equality must inevitably be more apparent than real. There is evidence that even in husband-and-wife teams where both are paid, the wife often emerges as the junior partner (Epstein, 1971a). Where the 'team' consists in a wife's participation in her husband's work, a junior partner is the most she can possibly be, since her contribution is formally unrecognised and totally unpaid. Such 'partnerships' depend upon a wife's accepting her inferior status. Young and Willmott noted that their directors and wives often talked in terms of marital partnership, and 'if the wife could accept that she was a junior partner, all could be well' (Young and Willmott, 1973, p. 258).

Despite the fact that she is unpaid, the contribution of a wife in such a 'team' can of course be of considerable value, not only to her husband, but to the organisation or enterprise which employs him. Thus, although a wife sees herself as working in partnership *with her husband*, her activities are directly of benefit *to his employer*. Writing of the country police forces, Cain comments that 'the policeman's work is greatly facilitated if he and his wife are accepted *as a team* by the people on the beat' (Cain, 1973, p. 127) (italics original); and Moorhouse writes of embassy life: 'An ambassador's wife is as crucial to a mission's success, in many ways, as is her husband himself . . . generally her influence is much less direct than the man's, a great deal of it exerted in the relationship which she has with other wives in the mission, with a consequent effect on everyone's morale' (Moorhouse, 1977, p. 258). Moorhouse is not a sociologist; but if his description represents something of the social reality of embassy life, the picture is one of a firm structure of social control within the embassy community, in which the ambassador's wife has a key position. Thus there are circumstances in which a wife's participation in her husband's work can concern not only clients, but also his colleagues.

Whatever the particular form which her participation takes, and whether she works alongside her husband or instead of him, these examples of wives' direct contributions to their husbands' work demonstrate clearly that many employers do indeed get two for the price of one, in that they benefit from the input of labour from someone whom they do not employ. Where the labour is contributed to the self-employed man, he himself is the main beneficiary. One need only look at the acknowledgement page of most academic books, for example, to see the extent of the debt which most men claim to owe their wives (Fowlkes, 1980, p. 72). In the past, such contributions seem often to have been deliberately kept secret. The biographer of Charles and Mary Booth notes that Mary did a great deal of work on *The Life and Labour of the People of London*, but had 'stipulated that her intensive work on Charles' volumes must be kept absolutely secret, but of course the other secretaries knew' (Norman-Butler, 1972, p. 134). More recently, a letter to *The Times*, following the death of Mrs Q. D. Leavis, the wife of the literary critic, observed that most people did not realise that she was a 'major collaborator in a number of books attributed to F. R. Leavis alone', and that lack of acknowledgement was not entirely welcome to Mrs Leavis herself (*The Times*, 26 March 1981).

Whilst the customary expressions of gratitude to one's wife in the acknowledgements of books by male authors may be entirely sincere, they may also mask contributions which, if made by anyone other than a wife, would have to be acknowledged and rewarded in more explicit ways. As such, they provide good examples of the outcome of marital 'partnerships', in which the husband's contribution is the one recognised in the public domain, and a wife's, if recognised at all, is acknowledged *through him*. Although the content of the example is rather special, the social processes which underlie it are not. The evidence reviewed in these chapters would suggest that it is not a serious misrepresentation of the social reality of most marriages.

11
The Productive Work of Wives

In analysing the ways in which wives contribute to their husbands' work, it has been possible to characterise these activities as peripheral and central, direct and indirect. The *possibilities* for a wife's incorporation do vary with different occupations: the *processes* through which such incorporation occurs are not straightforwardly occupation-specific. Some wives contribute more than others, but that primarily is a matter of opportunity. Almost all wives contribute *something* through their performance of domestic labour, which both services and frees the male worker.

So far the argument has been conducted at an individual level: *a wife* contributes to *her husband's* work. That indeed is how it is usually experienced and is, it will be argued, a significant part of the process through which such contributions are elicited. But if the issue is addressed at the collective level, one is examining the contribution of wives to social and economic production. The possibility seems to exist for a wife to make such a contribution whatever the relations of production under which her husband works: whether, for example, he is self-employed, a capitalist employer, or a wage labourer for the state. Although it would be very important to distinguish between these in other contexts, from a wife's point of view there is little difference between them since, it will be argued, the relations of production under which a wife contributes her vicarious labour are different from those in which her husband operates. So at this point, the argument returns to the issues raised in Chapter 1: in what sense do wives *as wives* contribute to production?

One way of viewing the incorporation of wives into their husbands' work is that it involves exploring the boundaries between paid and unpaid work, and between productive and domestic labour. In so doing, it both calls into question the place at which those boundaries are conventionally drawn, and challenges the significance usually accorded to them.

Although some writers on domestic labour would take the view that
it is not productive labour, at least not in the technical sense (for
example, Gardiner, 1976, p. 114), it is more consistent with the
evidence reviewed in this study to adopt the alternative position, that
housewives are in fact engaged in a form of 'private production within
individual families' (Himmelweit and Mohun, 1977, p. 15), and that
'domestic labour is of utmost *productive* importance to the capitalist
economy' (Middleton, 1974, p. 198) (italics original). So wives
contribute to production first, and importantly, through their
performance of domestic labour. But examples of wives' indirect
direct contributions are by no means confined to domestic labour, and
these provide some quite unequivocal examples of productive labour
being performed in domestic settings for a *husband's* employer, and
without direct remuneration.

The conventional distinctions between domestic and productive
labour handle these instances rather badly. Is a wife not really engaged
in productive labour if she does not receive a wage, or if she is not
working for an employer, or if the work is performed in the domestic
setting (Eichler, 1980, pp. 100–13)? Clearly none of these precludes a
wife from contributing to the processes of social and economic
production, if she does it vicariously through her husband. Should we
then draw the line at another point, and say that some examples of
vicarious work so obviously contribute to production that they have to
'count' (like typing a report), but that others where the relationship is
less direct (like taking on additional child care so that your husband
can type the report) will not count? Again, this seems unsatisfactory,
since the end result is the same: the intensification of the wife's labour
enables more of the husband's work to get done. Christine Delphy has
explored this kind of area in relation to her discussion of French
farmers' wives, an example which, it should be clear from this study,
does not represent such a unique experience as others have claimed
(Barrett and McIntosh, 1979, p. 100). Delphy argues that

> The example of self-consumption on the small farm illustrates
> clearly that there is no essential difference between activities which
> are said to be 'productive' (like fattening a pig) and domestic
> activities which are called 'non-productive' (like cooking the
> self-same pig) . . . 'Productive' use-values are no different from
> 'non-productive' use-values created by the purely domestic labour
> of the housewife. They are both part of the same process of creation
> and transformation of raw materials . . . and have the same goal:
> own-consumption.   (Delphy, 1977, p. 8)

So the conventional productive/domestic and paid/unpaid distinctions have comparatively little significance for wives who are incorporated in their husbands' work. They are *part of* the productive process even if they never leave the home for the purposes of work, and their labour is contributed although there is no direct wage relationship between them and the employer for whom, effectively, they work. Thus the productive and the domestic spheres are inextricably linked, and there is, for wives, no straightforward relationship between performance of productive labour and receipt of a wage. It is for this reason that the self-employed do not necessarily represent a unique example: in terms of a wife's relationship to production, being married to a self-employed man may be little different from being married to some wage labourers. To argue that 'the entrepreneurial family functions quite differently from the normal Western pattern' (Scase and Goffee, 1980, p. 90) is to miss that point.

The idea that work does not 'count' as part of economic production if it does not entail payment has already been strongly challenged in another context by the development of studies on the so-called informal economy (for example, Burns, 1975; Pahl, R.E., 1980; Gershuny and Pahl, 1980). The designation of *non-paid* activity as *non-economic* activity is one of the mechanisms which obscures wives' contributions to production via their husbands' work. Analysis of informal economy has begun to demonstrate the absurdity of that designation, and once it has more effectively penetrated the sociological consciousness, perhaps the importance of wives' vicarious contributions to production will become more self-evident.

Moreover, the organisation of production seems to *depend* very significantly on the incorporation of a wife's labour, which provides gratuitous additional input to the productive work in which her husband engages either as a wage labourer or on his own account. This input is very efficient. Not only is it given at no extra cost, but it is more flexible and more easily available as and when required than any other form of additional labour which one might envisage. The family wage, therefore, keeps not only a wife who contributes to production by servicing the male worker (McIntosh, 1978, 1979); in many cases it also keeps a spare worker, from whom labour can be extracted at no additional cost.

Some forms of work organisation afford more opportunities than others for the use of this spare worker, and some employers seek quite actively to use her. An interesting concept to consider here is Coser's notion of the 'greedy institution' (Coser, 1974). His argument is that, although a basic feature of contemporary societies is that most social institutions are limited (by law and in other ways) in the demands that they can make legitimately upon an individual, there are certain social groups which 'in contradiction to the prevailing principle, make total claims upon their members, and which attempt to encompass within their circle the whole personality. These might be called *greedy institutions* . . . Their demands upon the person are omnivorous' (ibid., p. 4). Although there are problems here with implied reification of 'the institution', it is interesting to consider Coser's point in relation to work organisations and employees' wives. Although the point remains relatively unexplored in Coser's own analysis, it would be hardly surprising to find that institutions with omnivorous tendencies seek also to extend their operations to wives; if only, on Coser's own analysis, to reduce the possibility that other relationships will make claims which conflict with their own demands (ibid., p. 6). Thus the incorporation of wives into the employing organisation, and the encouragement of their identification with it, serves to strengthen male employees' ties to that organisation. The British diplomatic service, according to Callan, 'takes for granted an unbounded commitment on the part of its employees and also of their wives' (Callan, 1975 p. 97); and the wife of an American soldier is advised that 'when a man enters the service, the government has gained not one but two – the man and his wife' (Dobrofsky and Batterson, 1977, p. 675). Similar examples could be replicated across a number of occupations, including not only the hierarchically organised, but also those where a man works as an independent professional or entrepreneur, such as wives of politicians or of the clergy, whose wives all express strong identification with their husbands' work. Sometimes the incorporation of wives into a hierarchical organisation becomes semi-institutionalised, and thus officially recognised, for example, as when senior diplomats' wives are allowed access to official transport. A similar kind of semi-institutionalised incorporation was evident in the report on army welfare, when it recommended that officers' wives who still wanted to play a welfare role should be eligible for training: 'if they wish, wives of commanding officers should be eligible to attend at public expense the Family Studies course at the University of Bristol' (Ministry of Defence, 1976, para. 400).

These examples begin to clarify two key features of wives' contributions to production. First, the organisation of productive work actually *depends* – in some cases very significantly so – on the assumption that wives' labour can be incorporated. Secondly, however, such incorporation is achieved – and perhaps can only be achieved – through a particular form of *marriage* relationship, which ensures that contributing to her husband's work has an unquestioned priority for a wife.

The material and cultural form of contemporary marriage is central therefore to the processes of incorporating wives' labour, in so far as it produces wives who are willing, even eager, to contribute their unpaid labour to their husbands' work. The reasons why contemporary marriage typically takes that form are discussed more generally in Part Three. In addition, however, a general willingness to contribute may be considerably reinforced by possible sanctions against those who do not comply. At its most basic, one sanction can be potential loss of livelihood. As Festing says, of the wives of Norfolk fishermen, 'Since their livelihood depended on it, they were involved in their husbands' work' (Festing, 1977, p. 151).

There may be comparatively few examples of direct loss of livelihood through a wife's non-participation, but probably many more where this sanction operates as a fear that the husband's present work and/or his future prospects might be *harmed*. Wives of politicians who fail to take on public roles are seen as injuring their husbands' performance (Papanek, 1973, p. 862). Wives of the clergy believe that they will damage their husbands' ministry if they fail to participate in it (Spedding, 1975, ch. 11). The social contribution of diplomats' wives is regarded as indispensable, despite the fact that bachelor diplomats of either sex are 'only mildly inconvenienced by their station' (Callan, 1975, p. 95). Soldiers' wives are constrained both in word and action by their potential reflection upon their husbands. As one American wife expressed it,

> Being a military wife, one must be careful in expressing an opinion because the outcome can be unhappy results for the husband. One is not an individual when married in the service, only an extension of one's husband, not only in body but also in mind.
> (Dobrofsky and Batterson, 1977, p. 678)

The very possibility of harming one's husband's work provides a powerful sanction against a wife' failure to contribute to it, not least because her future status and income are so dependent upon his (see below, chapters 12 and 13). Moreover, there is a sense in which that kind of failure would be regarded not only as a failure in his work, but also a failure in marriage, since she is not being a helpmeet. As well as the possibility that this will be regarded as personal failure, presumably the implied sanction of divorce lurks in the background: a wife who fails to perform adequately as a helpmeet may run the risk of being replaced by a more suitable model. Small wonder, then, that very few wives of managing directors or of clergymen are in full-time employment (Young and Willmott, 1973, ch. X; Spedding, 1975, ch. 11), or that the employment of wives is such a contentious issue in the diplomatic service (Callan, 1975, pp. 96–8): the development of independent work commitments among these wives might mean not only that less *time* was available, but also that their *commitment* to their husband's work could be undermined.

Examining the available sanctions perhaps makes the processes related to wives' incorporation seem more explicit than they appear in practice. For the most part, the fact that wives are contributing their labour to social and economic production is obscured, and the main way in which this is achieved is through the socially and ideologically constructed separation of work from home. The belief that the productive and domestic spheres are separate arenas in social experience, and that they can be considered as distinct conceptually, is a socially constructed belief precisely because it does not fully accord with material reality, where (as has already been demonstrated) the boundaries are much less distinct. However, the construction of the two spheres as separate has very important social consequences. First, it is crucial in creating the invisibility of women from the public domain, by assigning them to the domestic sphere, and designating that sphere as private. Thus women are systematically excluded both from public social life and from analyses of it. 'Women do not naturally disappear, their disappearance is socially created and constantly reaffirmed; often men's solidarity is created precisely on the basis of absence of women. Keeping women out of public roles is in fact a positive and time-consuming aspect of social organisation' (Edholm, Harris and Young, 1977, p. 126). Secondly, because the domestic sphere is treated as private, the notion that it *ought* to be private penetrates cultural practices, including the law: 'the courts are traditionally unwilling to interfere in a marital relationship . . . Behind this lurks the idea that, since husband and wife are a unit, their domestic life is a private world in which the law must not intervene' (O'Donovan, 1979, p. 141). This means that the conditions under which social relationships (of all kinds) in the domestic sphere are conducted remain not only relatively invisible, but relatively unregulated: 'the conditions of domestic production are relatively unregulated . . . there is no enforcement of payment for it' (ibid., p. 142). Thirdly, the exclusion of women from the public sphere produces accounts of womens' lives which make it appear that they have no independent social relationships outside the family, except through their husbands (Edholm, Harris and Young, 1977, pp. 125 ff). This helps to legitimate the pattern of vicarious relationships and make it appear natural (see below, pp. 153–7).

So the presumed separation of the public and private spheres not only obscures important features of wives' relationship to production, but it actually creates key features of the conditions under which that activity takes place. It constitutes the location of their vicarious work as a sphere which is private and in which others should not interfere, where women and the relationships under which their labour is extracted are invisible to other people (and perhaps most importantly, to other women) and where it seems both legitimate and natural that their relationships to social and economic production should be conducted at second-hand, through their husbands. The 'location' of wives' vicarious contributions in the domestic sphere in this context means most importantly within the marriage relationship. Many such contributions are of course made within the physical confines of the home, but they do not have to be. Wives of politicians who go on campaign tours, clergymen's wives who run church women's groups and wives of publicans who serve in the bar each lunchtime are all contributing vicariously to the productive activity in which their husbands are engaged – even if the production is of services rather than goods. Although their contributions are not made *in* the home, they are made in the ideologically constituted 'domestic sphere', because their character derives from the context in which they are made – that is, the marriage relationship. They are if anything slightly more visible than contributions made in the home, but their character as vicarious contributions remains the same.

A further important feature of this socially constructed separation be-tween work and home, and the context which it creates for wives, is that it makes a wife's vicarious contributions *to production* look as if it is work done *for her husband*. Of course in one sense the work *is* done for her husband. To anticipate the argument developed more fully in Part Three, it makes sense for a wife to contribute to her husband's work and generally to facilitate it because, given other constraints, in-vesting *in him* is one way in which she can hope to derive benefits her-self. Moreover, the work is done in a context where she has no direct relationship to an employer, and where it is all conducted via her husband. This means that wives' contributions are not made straightforwardly in a wage relationship (although wives may seek to derive economic benefits thereby), and therefore the relations of production under which *her* labour is extracted are somewhat different from the relations of production within which her husband works.

One way of conceptualising this would be to follow Delphy at this point, and to argue that the relations of production under which a wife's vicarious contributions to her husband's work are extracted are patriarchal relations, seen as a natural consequence of the marriage relationship:

> marriage is the institution by which gratuitous work is extorted from a particular category of the population, women-wives. This work is

gratuitous for it does not give rise to a wage but simply to upkeep. These very peculiar relations of production in a society that is defined by the sale of work (wage-labour) and products, are not determined by the type of work accomplished.

(Delphy, 1976, p. 77)

Delphy's work on this issue has been the subject of considerable debate, especially on the question of whether, because 'the wage labourer sells his labour power [but] the married woman gives hers away' (Delphy, 1977, p. 15), this should be considered as a separate, so-called domestic mode of production (Barrett and McIntosh, 1979, pp. 98–9; Delphy, 1980, pp. 92–5). From the point of view of this study, the issue is not so much how to conceptualise a mode of production, but the importance of recognising that the relations of production under which wives work are very different from those of wage labourers. On this point, Delphy's critics are in complete agreement with her: 'no-one would want to deny that domestic work is private and involves very different relations of production from wage work and that this, rather than the nature of the work or the nature of the product, gives it a distinctive character' (Barrett and McIntosh, 1979, p. 98). It is, in other words, not the tasks performed which give the productive work of wives its distinctive character, but the particular relations of production under which they are performed.

One way of mapping out the distinctive character of wives' work, and especially of their labour incorporated in their husbands' work, is to ask the simple question: who benefits from it?

Major beneficiaries clearly are those who eventually own the product of her labour: her husband's employers. Women effectively work for nothing for employers whom often they have never met, and who have very few formal responsibilities towards them, save some responsibility to provide widows' pensions, which they would have to do whether or not an employee's wife has vicariously contributed her labour to their productive enterprise. None the less, employers readily assume that they can rely upon wives' making such contributions. There is, as Callan says in relation to the diplomatic service, the 'premiss of dedication', which is 'as much moral as it is occupational' (Callan, 1975, p. 97), and the assumptions which it contains are more about marriage than they are about employment. It is the crucial assumption that a wife will be committed to *her husband's* work upon which employers so commonly rely.

The assumption that they can rely on this commitment not only means that they can expect gratuitous imput of a wife's direct labour, but also that they can expect her to go on producing a well-serviced worker for their use. The importance of this is well recognised by employers. In this context their active interest in the 'welfare' of the wives and families of employees takes on a different meaning. A good example is the concern shown in both the army and navy welfare inquiry reports about the effects of periods of separation upon soldiers' and sailors' marriages. A study undertaken in connection with the report on navy welfare found that naval wives were significantly more prone to depression than other wives and that where children had displayed problems which led to their being referred to a child guidance clinic, those problems were significantly related to one parent's absence from home: 'as far as problems in the children are concerned . . . the problems that they exhibit are those of the loss of a parent and the reaction by the mother to the difficulties experienced, either because of feeling unsupported when the husband is away, or because of problems which they have when the fathers return home where there are several emotional conflicts about who should be boss in the home' (Ministry of Defence, 1974, p. 155). One of the recommendations of this report was that 'the maximum period of separation should be reduced to six months at the very earliest opportunity' (ibid., para. 25). Similar concerns were expressed in the report on army welfare (Ministry of Defence, 1976).

No doubt this denotes a quite 'genuine' concern for the hardships imposed upon individuals, but concern to preserve service marriages accords also with the interests of the services themselves. Lest this should seem too cynical an interpretation of the military's interest in welfare, its goal is made quite explicit in the army's report: 'Above all we recognise that the goal of high morale in the British Army, which depends for its manpower on the recruitment and retention of volunteers, is the proper objective of welfare' (ibid., para. 6). The links between morale, welfare and support for family life are traced out more explicitly in Goldman's study of the American military: 'The family is a device for accommodating the strains of military life, and family instability is linked to the exodus of those who do not fit in' (Goldman, 1973, p. 907). To this end, 'the military has organised itself to assist family life and elaborate programs involving professionals and volunteers have become necessary' (ibid.).

To put the point more generally, from an employer's point of view family life is good for the enterprise, since it produces male employees interested in working hard and earning money, whose physical needs are catered for at no additional cost, and when needed, it provides wives who will help to create cohesiveness and oil the wheels of the employing institution. A similar point has been developed in a very interesting way by Dorothy Smith, as part of her argument that corporate capitalism produces a very specific form of middle class alienation. This occurs because the middle class family stands in a sub-contractual relationship to corporate capitalism, and a wife's part in this contract is the production of a home with a particular moral and material character (Smith, 1973). Smith's argument is discussed more fully elsewhere (see below, pp. 127–8), but it is mentioned here to underline the argument that the incorporation of a wife's vicarious labour is of benefit to her husband's employer. In some occupations, her incorporation is not only beneficial but virtually essential to the enterprise.

Employers clearly do benefit from wives' incorporation, but husbands benefit as well. Sometimes of course the two are conflated, where the husband is self-employed, and thus derives benefit from his wife's labour as 'employer', whether or not her work for him entails a wage relationship. But where husbands themselves are wage labourers – whether engaged in producing goods or services, whether engaged in manual or mental labour – *they* derive benefits from their wives' incorporation in their work.

Indeed, a judiciously chosen wife can bring benefits to her husband's work even without the performance of specific tasks: quite literally, she is an *asset*. Marceau has argued, in relation to her study of French upper middle class couples, that wives bring social, economic and cultural capital to a marriage, which husbands can then use to assist their career advancement (Marceau, 1976, especially pp. 206–11). Developing the same kind of argument from the viewpoint of an economist, Benham has analysed marriage in terms of the accumulation of human capital within the household. He argues that substantial capital accumulation is associated with marriage to a well-educated woman, and that the benefits (as measured by increased income) will be reaped by her husband in the labour market (Benham, 1974).

Sometimes couples adopt a very explicit strategy of using a wife's labour to enhance her husband's market position, especially through additional training, and perhaps entailing the denial of her own career prospects. This was recognised by Parsons, in his discussion of the Normal American Family, where he discusses the P.H.T. phenomenon: the process whereby young married women provide financial support to Put Hubby Through college or graduate school (Parsons, 1970, pp. 197–8). This is a somewhat risky enterprise, which can rebound on a wife in a number of ways. Beverley Jones has suggested that it may result in husbands being embarrassed at their wives' comparative lack of education: 'He forgets that his cultivation took place at his wife's expense. He will not admit that in stealing from his wife her time, energy, leisure and money, he also steals the possibility of her intellectual development, her present, her future' (Jones, 1970, p. 54).

So, by the capital which she brings to a marriage, by making direct and indirect contributions, and by her performance of domestic labour, a wife facilitates her husband's performance as a worker, thus enhancing his present performance and his future potential. To anticipate somewhat the discussion in Part Three, this indeed is one of the reasons why it makes sense for her to do it: by enhancing her husband as a worker, she hopes indirectly to gain. But the benefits as well as the contributions are always second-hand: she cannot benefit without his benefiting also, and the gains for him may be greater than for her. First, if his earning capacity is thereby enhanced, the increased money will be *his*, with no guarantee that all or some of it will be passed on to her. Secondly, if his status or prestige is enhanced, she may bask in the reflected glory, but the whole point about that is that it is *reflected*, and the prestige reflected on to a dependant remains a pale imitation of that accorded to the central character (Eichler, 1973, p. 46).

Thus both husbands and employers benefit from the incorporation of a wife's labour. It would be difficult to work out, except in particular circumstances, which of them derives the greater benefit, but what seems clear is that wives themselves come a rather poor third. Even such benefits as they do derive (enhancing their husbands' earning capacity, the vicarious status accorded to themselves, and so on) are acquired in a context which confirms, and often reinforces, their status as economic and social dependants. Furthermore, they can only continue to derive those benefits, not simply by the continued input of their labour, but by remaining within the particular marriage relationship.

So the benefits to a wife are, to say the least, ambiguous. A discussion of why it still makes sense for wives to make these contributions forms a major focus of the final part of this book.

Married to the Job: the Foundations of Wives' Incorporation

Introduction to Part Three

The aim of this concluding section is, in drawing together the analyses developed in Part One and Two, to locate discussions of the two sides of wives' incorporation in wider debates, identifying especially those parts of the analysis which develop and diverge from previous accounts.

To return to the issues posed in Chapter 1, one context within which a discussion of wives' incorporation needs to be located is in debates about the intersection between work and family in contemporary societies, and at the most general level, that means primarily the relationship between capitalism and patriarchy expressed in a particular household form (see, for example, J. Mitchell, 1971, ch. 8; Secombe, 1974; Harris, 1977; Beechey, 1979). That is, how far does the organisation of the capitalist productive process require a particular family form (typically characterised as the geographically mobile nuclear family with one male wage-earner and one female domestic labourer), and how far does capitalism make the family peripheral to production?

The evidence of this study seems to lend credence to the view that there is a powerful congruence of interest between the organisation of productive work and a family form in which a wife not only services the worker, but also (one should add) is available to contribute to production through him. That observation, however, does not necessarily imply a view of the family simply as a dependent variable of capitalism. Accounts of the relationship which concentrate on a simple notion of 'fit', and then argue that a particular family form exists because it 'serves the needs' of capital, are subject to all the well-known criticisms of functionalist accounts (Morgan, 1975, ch. 1), even if they are couched in Marxist, or indeed feminist, terminology (Barrett, 1980, pp. 188–9). The consideration of wives' incorporation in men's work suggests two particular kinds of problems with accounts which assume a simple 'fit' between capitalism and the family and, in identifying those problems, suggests way in which such accounts need to be modified.

First, functionalist accounts of all types, as is well known, leave no room for individuals to be social actors, or to take any part in shaping and making sense of their own lives. The account presented here suggests that it is not only possible but also necessary to do that, in order fully to understand the processes of wives' incorporation. Wives are not simply passive recipients of orders from capitalist employers, channelled through their husbands, which they are powerless to do other than to obey. Rather, it will be argued that the evidence suggests a model in which wives create a pattern of incorporation out of materials available to them, which may include received messages, but which also include their own understanding of what constitutes a marriage, and of the costs and benefits to themselves in making certain investments in their husbands' work. In other words, wives actively co-operate with their own incorporation because it makes very good sense to do so. This is not to deny that someone else reaps the benefits of their labour, nor that some completely different arrangements might be more satisfactory for most women. But it *is* necessary to produce an account which recognises the fact that most women do not experience their incorporation as unwelcome or alienating, and an account which does not imply that it occurs simply because women are too stupid to recognise their real situation. Thus, although many of the questions suggested by other writers (see the discussion in Chapter 1) raise issues of wives' incorporation at the structural level, an adequate analysis needs also to address the issues at the level of social interaction. Hence the discussion in these concluding chapters attempts to look at both, and at their inter-relationship.

Secondly, over-simple accounts of the fit between capitalism and the family gloss over the very real differences *between* families in this respect. This study has highlighted a number of differences, and it will be argued that the most significant ones occur along the occupational dimension; that is, the ways in which work tasks are organised in different occupations have radically different implications for the worker's wife (see below, pp. 130–1). Accounts which talk of work–family relations as if they were more or less the same for everyone are far too crude to take this into account, and need to be modified to capture the subtleties which result.

The same applies to the terms often set for the debate about whether the development of capitalism has the effect of removing the family from the centre of economic and social life, and making it peripheral to production. Again, the terms in which the question is posed are too crude. On the evidence of this study, some families are more peripheral to production than others.

The three chapters in this concluding section concentrate on spelling out the complexities, the context and the meaning of being married to the job. Chapter 11 explores the varieties of form which wives' incorporation takes, and relates those to the kind of work done by men. The final two chapters address the question: why is it that wives continue to be available for incorporation? Chapter 12 examines possible answers at the macro or collective level; that is, the ways in which social and economic life is organised effectively to produce this particular outcome. In Chapter 13 the same question is explored at the micro level, looking at how it comes to make sense for wives to accept their incorporation.

12

Varieties of Incorporation and the Occupational Dimension

The point that wives get incorporated in their husbands' work in different ways, and that those ways are crucially related to men's occupations, has been well illustrated in Parts One and Two. The aim of this chapter is to look more generally at the relationship between forms of incorporation and the occupational structure, to see how far variations can be accounted for by the type of work done.

Of course, not all forms of incorporation depend on the type of work done. Indeed one of the central themes of this study has been that *all* wives (except in very unusual circumstances) are incorporated to some degree. The most general forms of wives' contributions are through domestic labour and giving moral support. The most widespread effects of men's work *upon* wives' lives are felt through the level of material provision which it affords, through the timetables which it imposes and through the vicarious status which it assigns.

Beyond these important and widespread forms of incorporation, however, there is scope for forms which are both more intensive and more varied; and these do seem to be related in some way to the jobs which husbands do. It is therefore worth going back to some of the issues raised in Chapter 1, and examining more closely some arguments about the links between characteristics of work and wives' incorporation. The rest of this chapter considers the arguments that wives' incorporation is a special feature of professional and bureaucratic careers; that it is a special feature of middle class work; that it is related to the characteristics of particular occupations.

Professional and Bureaucratic Careers

The argument that wives' incorporation is a particular feature of professional and analogous work is the implication of Papanek's

(1973) important paper. Although she argues at the beginning that the two-person single career is not confined to middle class occupations (ibid., p. 825), her discussion draws on examples from professional and bureaucratic employment, where notions like 'career', 'achievement' and 'progression' provide the fundamental organising concepts for discussing work over time. So, is there something particularly significant about professional work *per se*, or about work which offers a clear career ladder, which accounts for the more intensive forms of wives' incorporation?

Certainly some forms of incorporation seem to occur most frequently in professional and bureaucratic careers. There are likely to be more opportunities to make direct contributions, for example, if one is married to a man who does professional work than to one who does factory work. Similarly, the structuring effects of a lifetime of geographical mobility are likely to occur where one's husband is trying to climb a career ladder. These, and many more examples, could be adduced from material already discussed.

There are however two important reasons for exercising caution in linking wives' incorporation with professional and bureaucratic careers, or at least for making those links in a simple way. The first reason is to do with matters of fact, the second with matters of theory.

First, on the basis of the empirical evidence already discussed, there seems to be virtually no form of wives' incorporation which is linked exclusively with professional and analogous work, except in matters of detail. Geographical mobility, for example, is not the sole prerogative of those groups although it is often treated as if it were. Some of the worst effects of it are probably experienced, for example, by soldiers' wives, because their husbands' moves are entirely outside their own control. Similarly, opportunities for making contributions are not confined exclusively to the wives of professionals. The publican's wife who chats to the clientele as she serves them, or the wife of the self-employed plumber who makes coffee for potential customers while they wait for her husband to return, are making the same *form* of contribution as the business executive's wife who cooks dinner for overseas customers. They are all attempting to create a socially congenial atmosphere which will be good for business; although certainly the detailed *content* of their activities reflects cultural designations of behaviour appropriate to different settings.

The second reason for rejecting a simple link between professional work and wives' incorporation is that there is a danger of reifying the notion of profession; that is, of treating a range of jobs as if there were something intrinsically distinct and special about them. To do so would be to ignore the whole critique which sees professionalism as a label which certain occupational groups claim, some successfully, others not

(Becker, 1971). So jobs which have successfully claimed the 'profession' label cannot properly be treated as if they shared some inherent quality which necessitates the incorporation of wives. On the other hand, one might argue that the process of claiming the label involves successfully establishing that the work entails a high degree of commitment, both on the part of the male worker and his family. Of course, it is not essential that the workers *actually* demonstrate such commitments, merely that they are believed to have them (Friedson, 1970, p. 81). So even if the organisation of professional work *per se* does not necessarily incorporate wives, there might be a case for arguing that the public ideology of being a professional does have that effect. Once the professional label is successfully claimed, it becomes part of the social reality within which the work is undertaken, and both the worker and his wife may need to take account of that.

There are links therefore between professional/bureaucratic work and forms of wives' incorporation, but they are not links unique to, or inherent in, that kind of work. In fact, those links can be specified much more precisely as features of the ways in which professional and bureaucratic work is commonly organised and publicly presented. So, in so far as professional/bureaucratic careers present career ladders which are facilitated by geographical mobility, offer opportunities for work to be done at home, are facilitated by the creation of a congenial atmosphere and promote a public ideology of service, they do imply possibilities for the more intensive forms of wives' incorporation. On the other hand, all of those features can be transposed to non-professional occupations with, it has been demonstrated, very similar effects.

Class Dimensions of Wives' Incorporation

The argument that middle class work provides special opportunities for wives' incorporation can take several different forms. Sometimes it can actually mean professional work. If one takes a broader definition of 'middle class' as 'non-manual' work, is there a case for regarding these occupations as more likely than manual occupations to facilitate the more intensive forms of wives' incorporation? Many of the examples discussed in Parts One and Two do cluster in the non-manual sector, but there are important exceptions, especially workers in the police and military services, where clear and significant examples of wives' incorporation are to be found. Furthermore, it has already been argued that wives of self-employed manual workers are often in an analogous position to wives of self-employed professionals, especially if they work at home. All of these would have to be regarded as exceptions if the manual/non-manual dichotomy were taken as the key one for wives' incorporation. So it appears that, to say the least, hierarchical status rankings of occupations do not provide a useful tool in the analysis of wives' incorporation.

A much more interesting variation on this theme is suggested by Dorothy Smith (1973) when she considers specific features of middle class work in relation to corporate capitalism. From the point of view of wives' incorporation in men's work, the key features of Smith's argument seem to be that the relationship of the middle class wife to economic production is fundamentally different from that of the working class wife. The difference is that middle class wives are oriented to an externalised order, which assigns them a place in the home where they identify with the values, standards and symbols by which social life is ruled, and manage their families in a sub-contractual relationship to corporate capitalism. Thus the middle class family 'is *for* the realisation of the ruling-class moral order' whereas the working class family 'is *for* its members' (ibid., p. 20).

Thus Smith's work shifts the emphasis of the argument away from definitions of class based on occupational hierarchies to definitions based on the relationship to the means of production. In this respect, her thinking is somewhat reminiscent of Engels's observation that the wife of the bourgeois is more oppressed than the wife of the proletarian because she is more subjugated to male supremacy (Engels, 1940, pp. 76–80). Although Engels's argument can be challenged on a number of grounds (Delmar, 1976; Kuhn, 1978), it points to important issues about the implications for wives of the different relations of production under which men work. Smith's view is that the implications are distinctive for wives of the middle class because corporate capitalism has created 'a second relation of alienation, the alienation of the bourgeoisie' (Smith, 1973, p. 11). A key part of this is 'The corporate structure requires of a manager that he subject himself and his private interests to the goals and objectives, the daily practices, and the "ethic" of the corporation. His *person* becomes relevant – the kind of person he is' (ibid., p. 20). The wife's part is to create and sustain that moral status which the corporation requires. In so doing, she may get into a double-bind where being 'a good wife' and working a curative effect on the injuries done to her husband in the occupational world, she may find herself supporting 'that very system which violates him' (ibid., p. 27).

Smith's work offers a useful insight into the special character of wives' incorporation when a family is, in her words, for the realisation of the ruling class moral order. However, on the basis of the evidence reviewed in this study, that would apply not only to families where the male breadwinner is employed by the institutions of corporate capitalism. The clergy and the police both provide good illustrations of families being oriented to the realisation of the ruling class moral order, but neither is related to corporate capitalism in a straightforward way. Indeed the latter, like the military, would not even count as middle class on any conventional definition, and there would seem a good case for arguing that certain employees of the state (employees who work in what would be described in other contexts as the repressive state apparatuses) experience the same kind of alienation as Smith outlines for the employees of corporate capitalism, and their families are similarly oriented to the realisation of the ruling class moral order.

So, modifying Smith's argument somewhat, it seems likely that wherever a family stands in a sub-contractual relationship to the ruling order, a wife's incorporation is given a particular character. This helps to explain, for example, why it is so difficult for a wife to compete for her husband's time against a job which is held to be of high social value.

There is therefore some significance for a wife in her husband's relationship to production, and the context in which he sells his labour power. However, this has to be set alongside the issue of a wife's own relationship. Of course she may also be a wage labourer in her own right, but *as a wife* what is her relationship to the means of production?

The implications of this study would tend to support the view that marriage makes a crucial difference to a woman's class position in that it puts her in the position where her labour can be vicariously incorporated. Remaining childless does not release a wife from this, although it may make it easier for her to counteract potential incorporation (for example, by keeping a full-time job and therefore being marginally less available) or to mitigate some of the structuring effects of her husband's work (for example, she is not reliant upon her husband to release her from the home in his non-work time).

So the entry into marriage is crucial because it places a woman in a situation where her labour can be appropriated by her husband, and through him, by his employer. Leonard has called marriage 'a relationship of total dependency: the man acquires a woman's labour, time, and baby, to be applied to whenever he needs, in so far as he can control/persuade her within certain legal and customarily defined parameters, in return for support and protection' (Leonard, 1980, p. 259). Part of the labour which he acquires, one might add, contributes to the enhancing of his own work, as Delphy makes explicit: 'the husband . . . can sell [his wife's labour] on the market as his own if he is, for example, a craftsman or farmer or doctor' (Delphy, 1976, p. 78). Delphy captures very well the essence of this aspect of the labour relationship between husband and wife: it is a relationship in which no payment is offered and none expected because it constitutes part of the hidden contractual relationship of marriage (Gowler and Legge, 1978). Significant amounts of labour are extracted from wives routinely without payment, and such is the socially constructed nature of the marriage relationship that it passes as unremarkable that a woman should perform tasks for her husband which, if she performed them for anyone else, would certainly require payment. Where I would differ from Delphy's analysis is that first, I would regard the incorporation of a woman's labour as much more routine and widespread than the specific examples which she discusses at this point. Secondly, I have argued that the husband is not always the sole, or even the main, beneficiary from his wife's input of labour, although no doubt he always does benefit. Examples of wives' incorporation occur not only amongst the self-employed, although the way in which self-employed work is organised may afford special opportunities. In other words, men who are wage labourers can and do sell their wives' labour as their own.

Since marriage puts a woman in this vicarious relationship to the means of production via her husband, there is a sense in which we have to say that marriage reconstitutes a woman's class position. This is not the place to repeat the analyses which have shown very effectively how profoundly unsatisfactory are existing concepts of class for handling the issue of women's class position (Acker, 1973; Morgan, 1975; West, 1978; Eichler, 1980), not least because those concepts have traditionally been formulated in relation to the public domain where women are invisible (Stacey, 1981). Whilst not attempting fully to engage with these debates, it seems reasonable to argue that the reconstitution of a woman's class position through marriage occurs because she is placed in a position in which her labour can be extracted through her husband and under patriarchal relations, whether or not she also sells her labour in the labour market, under capitalist relations of production. Thus a married woman's relationship to the means of production is more complex than a man's (or indeed than an independent single woman's) because it contains the additional element of vicarious extraction of labour, for which there is no male equivalent. Furthermore, a married woman's vicarious relationship to production does not simply replicate her husband's, since she has no control over the product of her vicarious investment of labour, whatever are the relations of production under which her husband works. Again Delphy is correct when she argues that the wife of a capitalist employer does not become a capitalist herself by her marriage: 'even though marriage with a man from the capitalist class can raise a woman's standard of living, it does not make her a member of that class. She herself does not own the means of production'

(Delphy, 1976, p. 15). To argue that the wife of a capitalist stands in the same relationship to production as the wife of one of her husband's employees is not to deny that in many ways the former may be better off than the latter. Higher income is no doubt inherently more desirable, and certainly the prospect of attaining it is one reason why wives continue to invest their labour in their husbands' work. But their attainment of higher income does not of itself alter their relationship to production.

So, to conclude this discussion of class dimensions of wives' incorporation, it seems that there *is* a case for seeing some of the more intensive forms of incorporation, especially those overlaid with an explicit moral character, as peculiar to men whose work identifies them with ruling class interests. However, this has to be set in the context of recognising, first, that the most widespread forms of incorporation are not class-linked; and second, that a man's class position is in any case of only limited significance for his wife, since her labour is vicariously extracted under quite different relations of production.

The Occupational Dimension

The occupational dimension has been a recurring theme in this study, and it is one which has not been given great emphasis by other writers. The term 'occupational dimension' refers not to the status of the occupation so much as to the content of the work and the way it is organised. Thus any single productive enterprise will encompass a number of different occupations whose content and organisation (and thus, their implications for the workers' wives) varies. This concept of an occupation accords with Everett Hughes's definition – 'the occupation is the place ordinarily filled by one person in an organisation or complex of efforts and activities' (Hughes, 1959, p. 445) – and with his view that an occupation implies a socially approved licence to carry out certain activities and a mandate to define the proper conduct of matters connected with work (ibid., p. 447).

Taking this perspective, the important question becomes: which specific features of the content of work and of work organisation have the most significant implications for wives' incorporation? That question needs to be looked at from both sides of the two-way relationship of incorporation, since the features which have the most far-reaching implications for imposing structures and constraints are not necessarily the same as those with the greatest power to elicit contributions, and vice versa. Posing the question in these terms should not be taken to imply a crude technicist explanation. Features of work organisation do not solely or straightforwardly produce wives' incorporation; but they do seem to shape the *form* which that incorporation is likely to take.

Mortimer, Hall and Hill (1978) do begin to unravel some occupational features which constrain wives' employment, but they tend to assume that professional work is especially significant in this regard, and some of their points effectively simply specify certain defining features of professional work (ibid., pp. 291–5). They do, however, usefully demonstrate that work which makes heavy demands on the worker's time, or which easily 'spills over' into non-work time, has particular implications for wives (ibid., p. 292). That conclusion would certainly be borne out by material considered in this study.

Taking it overall, what are the most significant features of work to emerge from this study? There seem to be five features of the way in which work can be organised which have especial importance both for structuring a wife's life and for eliciting her contributions. These are: flexibility of working hours; the possibility of work being done at home; living in institutional settings; work which is socially contaminating; and any kind of self-employment. These five must have pride of place for their ability to ensure the more intensive forms of wives' incorporation. In addition, work which entails frequent geographical moves or involves living in tied accommodation has special significance for structuring wives' lives. Wives are also likely to have contributions elicited if their husbands' job involves a certain amount of 'women's work' which can be conveniently siphoned off, or if his job is greatly facilitated by having someone with whom a message can be left at any time.

In spelling out the particular features of work like this, it becomes clear that the apparent association between wives' incorporation and professional work occurs because many of the most significant features are frequently associated with high status work. It is, however, those features rather than the status of the work which account for the different forms of wives' incorporation. Therefore, one would expect the implications for wives to be very similar wherever key features of their husbands' work organisation were similar, whatever the ranked status of that occupation. An empirical study which tested this out would be very interesting indeed: say, a comparison of wives of journalists and electricians who worked from home, or the wives of teachers in boarding schools, lecturers in residential colleges and prison officers in open prisons (assuming that all live in occupational colonies in relatively isolated settings).

Avoiding Incorporation

So the organisation of work tasks in particular occupations appears significantly to intervene in the relationship between work and the family, and creates crucial features of the way a wife relates to her husband's work.

In order to draw together the most significant features of men's work, this chapter concludes with an attempt to construct an advice list for prospective wives: an interesting, and not entirely frivolous, exercise. Let us suppose that a woman intends to marry, but wants to avoid (in so far as is possible) becoming incorporated in a man's work. We know that no wives can avoid this completely, but avoidance of the more intensive forms of incorporation should be possible if a husband is selected carefully. The most important rules to follow seem to be:

(1) Avoid a husband whose job entails frequent geographical mobility. You will hardly have time to start developing coping strategies in one place before you have to start all over again, and your chances of continuing your own employment in any satisfactory way are virtually nil. If you do have a mobile husband, try to make sure at least that his moves are at entirely predictable intervals, or that he has a considerable amount of discretion over the time when he makes each move.

(2) Any potential husband whose job has very flexible hours should be regarded with great suspicion. This will mean that you can never rely on his being at home, and therefore *you* will always have to be at home to cover domestic responsibilities. A nine-to-five man with plenty of holidays is a much better bet, because you can stand a greater chance of being able to get him to take on a regular share of child care and domestic work.

(3) If you want to try to work out shared domestic tasks, avoid a man whose job takes him away from home for blocks of time. This will mean that you have to take total responsibility for the home and the dependants whilst he is away. On the other hand, you may be able to turn this to your advantage – a man whose job takes him away from home should not be dismissed too hastily. You will have the great advantage of not having to take account of his work in the day-to-day organisation of your life, nor of servicing his daily needs, and this in itself removes many of the constraints to which other wives are subject. If you can develop good strategies for coping with the children without reference to him, a husband who is seldom at home (and then when he is at home, is not working) can be a very good prospect.

(4) Be very careful about going to live in a house which is in any way connected with your husband's work. You will have less control over your own home than most other people, and everyone else will quickly start to identify you as an appendage to your husband.

Worst of all is to go and live in an institutional setting composed of people with whom your husband works: you will then effectively become part of the hierarchy within which he works.

(5) Under no circumstances marry a man whose work is going to be based in your home, or even one who can work at home if he wants to. Not only will you never be able to rely on his being off work, but also you will have to organise the home *around* his work. The possibilities for your being sucked in are endless, and are very difficult to avoid when the work is being done at home.

(6) Beware the seductions of self-employment. Being your own boss may sound very attractive, but the man who employs himself often needs his wife's labour to make the business viable, and the rewards for you may be none too tangible.

(7) Avoid men doing work which contaminates the whole of their lives, work which is highly socially valued, or has strong moral overtones. You too will rapidly become contaminated and you will find it virtually impossible to compete with his work.

(8) Regard with great suspicion any man whose work entails certain tasks which look like women's work. If he has the discretion which enables him to siphon them off, he will off-load them on the nearest available and reliable woman – yourself. This will probably happen in the first instance when you help out in a crisis, but soon it will become routine.

If this advice is followed, a good many potential husbands will be excluded. However, should a woman manage to find a nine-to-five factory worker who has a job for life in the same place, there is no actual guarantee that she will be totally unaffected by his work. Indeed, even if she is, that in itself may not be entirely satisfactory. There is a fine piece of irony here: the kind of man to be avoided if you want to maintain maximum distance from your husband's work may well be precisely the kind of man most likely to fulfil that other culturally desirable attribute for a husband – being a good breadwinner. Moreover, the features of work which, from a wife's point of view, are to be avoided are often precisely the same features which the male worker himself may covert. Flexibility of hours, the ability to exercise a degree of control over your own work schedule and being able to work from home if you wish – these are all features of work organisation which create a working setting which is more congenial for the worker, and are often sought after. But at the same time, they are the precise features of work organisation most likely to hedge in his wife, leave her little room for manoeuvre, and to elicit gratuitous contributions from her.

13

Doing Three Jobs: the Hierarchy of Priorities

The purpose of the last two chapters is to examine the question: why do wives continue to be available for incorporation into men's work? Of course this is ultimately part of larger questions about why women continue to *marry* which, although beyond the scope of this study to explore fully, will inevitably be touched on as part of the specific discussion of incorporation. In this chapter possible answers at the macro level will be considered, by looking at how far one can argue that social life is organised in ways which produce that particular outcome.

The main theme of this chapter is that decisions about a wife's potential incorporation in her husband's work, and how that relates to her lifestyle, tend to become routinised in a rule of thumb which comes into operation when relevant issues arise. This rule of thumb is the work-family-work hierarchy. It is a hierarchy of priorities in which the needs of the husband's work are accorded top priority, followed by those of the family (primarily, but not exclusively, children), with a wife's own paid work, actual or potential, coming a very poor third. As Fowlkes puts it, family life 'takes its shape from and is contained by' the structure of the male breadwinner's work (Fowlkes, 1980, p. 173). Edgell alludes to this hierarchy (and one of the reasons for it) when, on the basis of his study of middle class couples, he argues, 'It is the wife (and children) who largely depend upon the husband for sustenance; and it is therefore the wife who tends to "accommodate" to the husband who in turn has to "accommodate" to the occupational system' (Edgell, 1980, p. 106). The hierarchy of priorities is maintained, it will be argued, by a variety of structural and cultural supports. The implication for wives who also have paid work is that they potentially carry the burden not simply of *double* labour (paid work and domestic work) but of *triple* labour, because they contribute to their husbands' work as well.

The argument in this chapter depends fundamentally on the

assumption that relationships between work and family are not symmetrical for men and women. In practice, sexual divisions within the household crosscut work–family relationships, and that intersection produces very different consequences for men and women. This has already been illustrated, for example in the discussion of who deals with the worker's 'needs' created in work (see above, Chapter 6), but the argument needs to be spelled out more clearly at this stage.

The notion of symmetry within the family as developed by Young and Willmott refers partly to the present arrangements of certain families, and partly to future trends as the authors see them, that is, they are optimistic about the prospects for the creation of greater symmetry between the tasks done by husbands and wives, both inside and outside the home (Young and Willmott, 1973, ch. X). Their own evidence for this claim is rather shaky. Their study has been criticised for under-representing families with young children and elderly dependants (Land, 1978, p. 281) and for placing excessive importance on one question only in the interview, then using a coding scheme which gives too much weight to men who helped with domestic work just on odd occasions (Oakley, 1974b, pp. 163–4). Neither do their predictions for the future seem to be supported by other studies. Cohen's study of mobile middle class families on a housing estate – precisely the kind of families where the symmetrical pattern should be in evidence if Young and Willmott are correct – demonstrates almost the reverse: wives are left almost in sole charge of the household while their husbands are away pursuing their careers. The author concludes that 'Career pressures kept the majority of husbands apart from their families for considerable periods of time at a stage in their families' developmental cycles when their wives were most in need of their support. The symmetrical model of the family, therefore, is not applicable here' (Cohen, 1977, p. 603). Again, Edgell's study of middle class couples 'supports the . . . claim that marital relationships remain highly segregated, unequal and husband-dominated' (Edgell, 1980, p. 104). In a more theoretical critique of the underlying model of social change in the notion of the symmetrical family, Frankenberg has argued that Young and Willmott implicitly work with a model which is too idealistic and too optimistic, and assumes 'a direct and unmediated effect of technology on behaviour' (Frankenberg, 1976, p. 28).

So the notion of symmetry in family relationships is a singularly unpromising one, both as analysis of the present and as futurology (Bell and Newby, 1976, pp. 165–7). In terms of the central concern of this study, it will be argued that the effects of a spouse's work for his or her partner is *not* symmetrical for husbands and wives. In practice, the intervention of sexual divisions in the work–family relationship means that wives are considerably more likely to be incorporated in their husbands' work than vice versa.

The asymmetrical nature of work–family relationships is recognised by a number of writers. Bailyn (1978), for example, discusses how the complex of the 'husband's work link/family link/wife's work link' is managed differently by different couples. In Fowlkes's study, where some wives of male academics were themselves doing academic work, a certain amount of reciprocal assistance did pass from husband to wife, but in ways which never challenged the centrality of the male career (Fowlkes, 1980, pp. 76–7).

In certain occupational examples the asymmetry is very clear. In those occupations, for example, where wives are incorporated primarily into an institutionalised social life and into entertaining, it is clear that *wives* not *spouses* are being incorporated, since the form of the incorporation entails the performance of traditional female social and domestic skills. The husband of a female executive or diplomat *could not* be incorporated in the same way: not because he would be incapable of demonstrating skills of domestic organisation and being a gracious hostess but because, if he did so, he would be engaged in a totally different activity. A wife who is a good hostess is fulfilling an understandable and socially approved role; a man who developed the skills of being a good hostess to his wife's clients or colleagues would be stepping radically out of line, as the very word 'hostess', with its use in the female form, betrays. Thus tasks which are superficially the same become different activities when performed by a male or a female spouse, because their social meaning changes.

So it is clear that a degree of asymmetry in work–family relations does exist. It is less obvious, however, whether its form varies, for example, in different occupations, and in what circumstances a greater degree of symmetry might be created. The asymmetry derives from the maintenance of sexual divisions in marriage, which in most cases form a 'given' part of the situation in which wives must handle their relationship to their husbands' work. To argue this is not to imply that a particular form of sexual division of labour between husband and wife is either inevitable or natural. As Edholm *et al.* have convincingly argued, 'The starting point for an understanding of the sexual division of labour must be a recognition of its complexity, of the multiple levels at which it functions . . . How is it that we can refer at all to "the" sexual division of labour when patently its context changes radically from one environment and historical period to another?' (Edholm, Harris and Young, 1977, p. 118). This recognition, however, does not preclude the examination of a particular form of sexual divisions, and their intersection with work–family relations as they exist for a particular social or cultural group, at a particular point in history.

The Hierarchy of Priorities

The diverse demands of a husband's work have to be handled and responded to in some way by his wife, and that response itself has to be handled within the context of a particular form of sexual divisions within the household. It is argued here that a wife commonly handles this intersection with reference to a hierarchy of priorities, in which her own needs take third place, behind the needs of her children which themselves are subordinate in the last resort to the demands of her husband's work. The way in which the scheme of priorities operates is discussed here primarily in relation to a wife's own paid work, although clearly other features of her lifestyle are similarly prioritised. Paid work has been selected for specific discussion for two reasons. First, it provides a counterbalance to the discussion in Parts One and Two where the working wife makes only brief appearances, primarily because the available empirical studies often concern women who are full-time housewives. Secondly, a wife's paid work provides the major critical case for exploring the notion of priorities in women's lives. If a wife's incorporation in her husband's work is simply a way of providing her with a 'link' into the public domain, or an optional extra for the housewife with time on her hands, then one might expect the working wife to be incorporated to a much smaller degree, since she has her own 'link' to the public domain, and indeed her own financial resources. Looking at wives' paid work, linked with domestic demands, therefore provides a way of testing the meaning of a wife's incorporation in her husband's work, and the strength and character of the social processes which produce it.

Evidence of the operation of the hierarchy which accords a husband's work top priority has, in effect, been adduced throughout this study so far and there is no need to repeat it. Many illustrations have been given of circumstances in which that scheme of priorities is operating so that wives, for example, have their choices about where they live or how they organise their daily lives closely circumscribed by their husbands' work, and have the time available to pursue their own interests (in employment or otherwise) curtailed by the contribution which they make to his work. This is not to imply that such a scheme of priorities is universal or inevitable, nor that it cannot be modified in certain circumstances, nor that it is explicitly agreed or even explicitly acknowledged. It is, however, what happens in practice in most marriages, even when some attempt is made to get away from it.

A sense of the pervasiveness of the pattern can be adduced by looking at some of the evidence about two specific situations. First, what happens when a wife's employment might begin to challenge the scheme of priorities? Secondly, what happens when couples explicitly try to adopt a different scheme?

The occasions when a wife's employment actually provides a challenge to the scheme of priorities are probably relatively rare. In most marriages, the implicit hierarchy is sufficiently strong to ensure that potential conflicts are avoided: actions on the part of the wife ensure that her life is modified, adjusted and perhaps her aspirations changed, so that she can continue to fit it around her husband's. Decisions about a wife's employment may assume that it has a fairly low priority right from the early days of marriage. Leonard comments, of the newly married couples in her study, 'Paid employment for wives is seen as something the woman may *choose* to undertake . . . [it is] seen as her responsibility to organise her domestic work around her outside duties if *she wishes* to do it' (Leonard, 1980, pp. 243–4) (italics original). This device, of making all decisions from the beginning of a marriage *within* the hierarchy of priorities, probably ensures that conflicts between the wife's and husband's work never arise. Should they do so, however, there is ample evidence that, where there is a conflict of interest, the wife's employment is relegated to a lower priority. This should be clear from the discussion of geographical mobility (see above, pp. 45–53), which means that wives almost always follow their husbands, even when they themselves hitherto had been pursuing a recognisable, even a quite prestigious, career. Thus Marceau found that the wives of her French middle class couples gave up their jobs with no secure new job offer when their husbands changed employment (Marceau, 1976, pp. 213–16), and Platt found that married women sociologists – a group who might be expected to be relatively enlightened in these matters perhaps – typically followed their husbands, and took the most interesting job they could find in the place where he ended up (Platt, 1976, p. 125).

Of course it may be argued that these examples are drawn from studies done in a relatively favourable economic climate, and that decisions now about a wife's employment may be made in a completely different context where couples have to plan more carefully if the wife is to find paid work. It would be foolish to assert otherwise without recent evidence, and contemporary studies of wives' employment decisions are urgently needed. However, there are good reasons to expect that the change has not neccesarily been all that radical in most cases, because of the strong structural and cultural supports for the hierarchy of priorities (discussed in the following section). Furthermore, decisions about what job (if any) a wife should have are embedded in the whole structure of sexual divisions in marriage: to reverse the hierarchy of priorities in job-seeking would challenge that.

So job-seeking provides an illustration of how potential conflict between the demands of husband's and wife's employment is avoided. Other illustrations can be found in the processes whereby wives fit their own work *around* their husbands', both practically and ideologically. The case of homeworkers provides a very clear example of the practical aspects of 'fitting around'. Indeed, it is in some ways the hierarchy of priorities taken to its ultimate conclusion, since homeworking provides a way for a wife to take paid employment *and* to continue to fully service the home (Hope, Kennedy and de Winter, 1976, p. 99). Other examples of fitting work around the home can be found almost wherever women take paid work. Purcell (1981) reports that semi-skilled women workers in an engineering factory organised their lives to fit around their husbands' and children, and this conclusion is supported by evidence of another study of married women working in food factories (Shimmin, McNally and Liff, 1981).

Examples of the practical 'fitting around' can be paralleled by examples of ideological 'fitting around' one's husband's work. In an interesting discussion based on American studies, Safilios-Rothschild (1976) suggests that various strategies are adopted to ensure that a wife's occupational status is kept somewhat below her husband's, if there is any prospect that it might begin to exceed his. Wives work only office hours, decline to take additional work home, or refuse extra responsibilities, for example. These strategies of course facilitate the practical fitting around, but they also ensure that a wife is unlikely to overtake her husband in their respective career progressions. As Safilios-Rothschild argues, 'wives' occupational roles have been acceptable as long as the wives' achieved status lines were lower (or could be perceived as lower) than those of husbands . . . [this] is clearly demonstrated by the anxious efforts of successful professional women to stay below their husbands' achievements' (ibid., p. 53). That conclusion is supported by the work of Poloma and Garland, who show that in those cases where a wife's income *is* greater than her husband's, the couple would explain that this is necessary to keep up family living standards. 'It was significant that no wife *wanted* to earn more than her husband, but some in fact did in order to meet the family's needs' (Poloma and Garland, 1971, p. 756) (italics original). There was, in other words, a high degree of ambivalence about any situation in which a wife appeared superior to her husband in terms of income and implied status. So it seems that wherever a wife's employment provides any kind of challenge to her husband's work – practical or otherwise – the common response is for features of the wife's work to be modified, which has the effect of ensuring that it continues to be accorded a lower priority.

What of situations where couples try explicitly to get away from this, and develop a rather different scheme of priorities? Evidence about this can be gleaned from studies of dual-worker families, where both husband and wife are committed to full-time work, and even to the pursuit of hierarchically structured careers. These are situations in which, Gowler and Legge argue,

> the hidden contract in conventional marriage cannot be assumed. The husband cannot assume his wife's automatic commitment to providing domestic back-up support for his career, any more than the wife can make this assumption about her husband . . . The assumptions behind the husband's and wife's work and family commitments, and the rules for organising them must, to be workable, become explicit.   (Gowler and Legge, 1978, p. 56)

Although they may be correct about issues becoming more explicit, available evidence about dual-worker families does not really support the suggestion that assumptions about who will support whom, and whose work takes priority, are renegotiated from scratch. As they recognise themselves, there is a remarkably consistent tendency for priorities and patterns of organisation to converge towards the conventional (ibid., p. 57). The conclusion is supported both by studies which focus on well-qualified women, and by those which consider dual-worker couples. Even wives who are 'fully committed' to women's careers may accept that they are not 'feasible' in practice (Fogarty, Rapoport and Rapoport, 1971, pp. 262–3), and even between 'egalitarian' couples, in the last resort decisions about work tend to revert to the traditional model of sexual divisions (Rapoport and Rapoport, 1976, pp. 324–38; Berger, Foster and Wallston, 1978).

So the work-family-work hierarchy of priorities is not only the scheme upon which most wives operate in practice; it is also the one to which those who try to establish less conventional schemes will revert, when pressed. Why is this pattern so pervasive? Although some might like us to believe that it is part of the natural order of human life, it is actually a pattern which is socially constructed and sustained: clearly, it is possible to envisage alternative ways of ordering the intersection between work–family and sexual divisions in marriage. So it is important to examine the structural and cultural supports which serve to sustain this pattern, in order to understand its pervasiveness.

Structural Supports

The conventional hierarchy of priorities is not inevitable, nor is it unambiguously promoted. There is, indeed, a sense in which women get mixed messages: it is good to be independent, to try to have a career, to think for yourself; but your children need you when they are young, it is attractive for women to be caring and submissive, a good wife is one who is supportive of her husband. The messages are mixed, but only certain patterns of response will receive institutional and cultural support. In looking at those supports for the work-family-work hierarchy, in a sense one is looking just at one part of the structure of supports for patterns of male domination and female submissiveness across a whole range of social relationships. Other writers have concentrated on different contexts to explore how far such patterns of relationships can be regarded as natural, inevitable, or self-chosen. Hanmer, for example, writing of male violence against women, argues that explanations have to be related to social structure, and that it is inadequate to see violence simply as a product of socialisation:

> Dominant ideology states that female submissiveness and dependency on the male are self-chosen. The liberal challenge to this view does not blame women so obviously for their difficulties, as female submissiveness-dependency, like male aggression, is said to be taught through childhood socialisation into sex roles . . . on their own [these] are inadequate explanations of human conduct based on domination and submission. (Hanmer, 1977, pp. 222–3)

The same point applies to the hierachy of priorities: explanations which are 'purely' cultural – those which rely on socialisation, for example – would be inadequate, if only because they fail to explain why particular patterns of sexual divisions within marriages receive institutional support, and others do not. So the main features of the structural supports for the conventional hierarchy will be considered before discussing the cultural supports, although in many ways the two cannot easily be separated.

The two major ways in which the conventional hierarchy of priorities is supported are through the operation of the labour market, and through state social policies. It is beyond the scope of this study to explore these fully, but interesting work in both areas has been developed in recent years, especially by feminist writers. I shall attempt no more than to draw out from this work the major points which relate to support for a hierarchy of priorities in which the male career is given primacy.

First, the operation of the labour market is predicated on the assumption of mobility of labour, especially in certain sectors (see above, pp. 59–60). Recent feminist writers have argued that the need for mobility, combined with the need for workers to be serviced within the domestic context, has produced a system in which the male wage is seen as a family wage, covering the costs of a wife's provision of full-time domestic servicing (McIntosh, 1978, 1979; Land, 1980). The operation of the family wage system is supported through state social and financial policies related to tax and social security (Land, 1976, 1980).

Secondly, the position of the female wage-earner in the labour market usually is considerably worse than that of men, for a variety of reasons which combine to keep women in a disadvantaged position: inequities in schooling, employment history interrupted through undertaking full-time child care and the care of other dependants, and active discrimination against women in employment – not least because of assumptions that women, and especially married women, are not serious about their employment (see, for example, Barker and Allen, 1976a; Mackie and Patullo, 1977; Snell, 1979). These of course work to the disadvantage of single women as well as the married (Chisholm, 1977), but in terms of the present study they do mean that a wife is, in most cases, likely to be a less viable and less lucrative breadwinner than her husband. In other words, marriage *per se* puts a woman in a disadvantaged labour market position (Burkitt and Rose, 1981). So an alternative hierarchy of priorities, which accorded her work a much higher status, could well be financially disadvantageous to all concerned.

Thirdly, the development of an alternative scheme of priorities is not viable for most women because of the lack of certain kinds of provided facilities. A couple who both wish to pursue employment have to take upon themselves the provision of child care, for example, and the care of other dependent members of the family. Studies of such families suggest that the logistics of organising this can be formidable (Rapoport and Rapoport, 1971, pp. 285–7). The lack of socialised child care facilities, coupled with the increasing lack of state-financed facilities for other dependants, have serious implications for any notion of equal opportunities for women (Finch and Groves, 1980). Coupled with the likelihood that the male partner is a more viable breadwinner than the female, they produce a situation in which wives are faced with little alternative than to take the main responsibility for domestic work and child care in order to facilitate their husband as the main breadwinner, fitting their own employment (if any) around those responsibilities.

Such are the powerful structural supports for the conventional hierarchy of priorities. They help to explain, for example, why wives almost always carry the major share of domestic labour (Chapter 5). These important structural supports are also reinforced by supports which are essentially cultural, although it will be clear that the two cannot be completely disentangled.

Cultural Supports

Cultural supports for the work-family-work hierarchy are varied and diverse. This section will consider the nature of those cultural practices, and the content of those ideologies, which seem most important in this respect. Again, in most cases, quite brief reference will be made to other work which elaborates these features.

Firstly, the non-viability of wives as main breadwinners, although structurally sustained is also culturally reinforced. While the cultural practice that women should 'marry down' (both in terms of age and status) remains it is virtually ensured that a wife will never be an equally viable breadwinner with their husband, still less a *more* viable one, barring some unusual circumstance such as his becoming disabled (Gillespie, 1972, p. 137). Moreover, once married, there is a good chance that a wife will fall further behind since, as Rossi has pointed out in relation to the American situation, well-qualified women who try to continue their careers will find that marriage, parenthood and advanced study are 'compressed into the same narrow few years in early adulthood' (Rossi, 1971, p. 111). In her view, the consequence is that 'There is not enough time in late adolescence for young women to evolve a value system of their own and a sense of direction towards an individual goal, for they are committing themselves prematurely to marriage and adapting to the goals of their husbands at the expense of their own emotional and intellectual growth' (ibid., p. 112). Although women may to some extent be able to sustain their comparative viability as breadwinners by delaying childbearing, this is unlikely to make a radical difference since the crucial issue is the assumption that a woman will withdraw from the labour market and be dependent upon her husband *at some stage*. The more radical choice *never* to have children remains very much a minority response and certainly is not an option likely to receive cultural approval.

Secondly, the effective exclusion of most women from some sectors of the labour market is reinforced by the operation of male occupational cultures, which serve to exclude women from key processes (and therefore from further advancement) should they succeed in breaking in. The widely recognised use of the male environments of pubs and clubs as a location for business dealings is just one example of this, not to mention the operation of old boy networks. An interesting early example was offered in a paper by Everett Hughes, written in 1945, which describes how a female aircraft designer did not take part in the male rituals surrounding the maiden flight of *her* plane (Hughes, 1958, p. 108).

Thirdly, there are important gender differences in whether one can treat work as a so-called 'central life interest'. This concept perhaps needs to be used with caution, since it implies a somewhat static view. An individual may, for example, treat work in this way early in adult life, but not later. Nevertheless, the concept captures an important facet of the way in which work can feature in the life of an individual: it can become a priority not simply in terms of time and organisation, but also in terms of identity. As such, work has been more often associated with male than with female workers (Hunt, 1980, p. 7). That is not to say that all men, or even most men, make work their central life interest. Indeed Dubin, in his key study, found that three-quarters of his male manual workers did not do so (Dubin, 1962). It is not so much a question of how many men actually do this, but rather that they are *allowed* to specialise in work, as it were, as their central life interest, whether or not they have spouse and children. Women, however, will find that they meet with much less cultural approval if they specialise in work, especially if they are also wives and mothers. Thus it is not surprising to find that when wives do work, the significance which that work has for them is less than for many men and is related to the context of marriage. This point is brought out very well in Stacey's two Banbury studies. Although there were more married women at the time of the second study than at the time of the first, the comparative *meaning* of work and family seemed to have changed little.

> Most women are still wives and mothers first. The most active area for women is still the family . . . the reasons given for a wife not going out to work related to the effect it was felt her employment would have on the family, rather than anything intrinsic to a job. Home-making and child-rearing remain the 'central life interest' of the majority of women in Banbury.
>
> (Stacey, Batstone, Bell and Murcott, 1975, pp. 105–8)

The importance of work as a source of personal identity seems as rare for married women as is the likelihood that they will be accorded social status in their own right. This is one consequence of making it possible for women to derive their central identity from their close personal relationships – by being a good wife and a good mother especially – in a way which men cannot. Thus women always have a socially approved alternative to work. Since it is difficult for women to sustain work as a central life interest on other grounds, it is not surprising that many women take that alternative, even if their qualifications might suggest otherwise. As Blackstone and Fulton, writing of male and female university teachers, observe, 'so long as men *must*, while women *may* have careers, there are a host of decision-points where men are sustained by the expectation that they will continue, while for women the decision to move on is problematic: they always have the option of abandoning their career for the socially approved role of housewife' (Blackstone and Fulton, 1975, p. 268).

Fourthly, there is a whole range of cultural practices which support the priority of family, especially of children, over a wife's employment. These are underscored by particular ideologies of motherhood. Only brief reference can be made here to the very interesting work which has been developed on this topic. In the context of the present study, the most important features seem to be: first, the emphasis on the needs of children which are said to include certain needs which only their own mother can supply; and secondly, the notion that motherhood itself is a *job*, an alternative to paid work, and an alternative which is intrinsically more satisfying for a woman.

On the first point, about the concentration on the needs of children, readers no doubt will be familiar with the very significant postwar influence of the work of Bowlby, which emphasised the centrality of full-time mothering to a child's development, and the challenges to it (Rutter, 1972, ch. 2; Oakley, 1974a, pp. 203–21). Those ideas have been important not least because they accord with implicit assumptions of motherhood embodied in state policies (Wilson, 1980, ch. 4). The strength of these ideas in practice could be illustrated in many ways. One interesting way is to look at what happens to practices of mothering when individuals and couples set out deliberately to establish a non-conventional lifestyle. Abrams and McCulloch's study of British communes shows clearly that, even in these settings, womem remain in a state of what they call 'social secondariness' and motherhood in particular remains 'an all-demanding and totally female role' (Abrams and McCulloch, 1976, p. 271). In the public arena, statistics collected by official agencies usually relate women's, but not men's, employment to family life (Oakley and Oakley, 1979, p. 183), thus demonstrating the taken-for-granted assumption that only women's paid work affects the family.

One consequence of this concentration on the centrality of the mother for the adequate social production of a child is to present women with clear choices *between* employment and full-time motherhood; and where they try to combine the two, to ensure that they have to be seen to be putting the needs of the child first. Moral panics about inadequate child care typically devolve upon mothers, and, as the Pahls comment when discussing the difficulties encountered by those of their managers' wives who wished to find work, 'her employers may suspect that she will not be fully committed to them, while neighbours may await the first signs of delinquency in her children' (Pahl and Pahl, 1971, p. 134).

So wives are faced with handling their ordering of priorities within a social context in which they are likely to experience strong social approval if they demonstrate that they are putting the needs of their children first; and the reverse if there is any hint that their own employment is assuming a high priority.

This concentration on the needs of children is paralleled by the notion that women are meant to find motherhood intrinsically satisfying – a state to which many women apparently aspire, despite experiences to the contrary (Oakley, 1979, ch. 11). In part this is because the comparative satisfactions to be derived from work and family are culturally designated as different for men and women – work is seen as more satisfying for men, family for women. Of course there are many situations in which experience does not bear this out: many men do jobs from which it is very difficult to derive intrinsic satisfaction, for example. None the less, the expectation that women will find work less satisfying than the production of children, combined with the emphasis on the importance of that production, ensures that a woman will be swimming against the tide if she attempts to reverse this particular scheme of priorities. This applies even to women who are qualified to do work which would be regarded as intrinsically satisfying work if done by men. Papanek, writing primarily with academic women in mind, puts it this way:

> Prevailing social stereotypes tend to require [a wife] to be satisfied with knowing the extent of her contribution to her husband's work and to the growth and development of her children. And who, indeed, should measure published output in books and journals against such tangibles as children? (Papanek, 1973, p. 861)

This insight of Papanek's captures well the dilemma in which the work-family-work hierarchy places a wife: it puts her in the position of having to justify herself if she does not find totally satisfying the production of children and support for her husband's work.

Finally, the conventional hierarchy of priorities is culturally supported by particular ideologies of marriage, which confirm a wife's secondary status. This is not so much a case of male domination and female subordination: it is actually more subtle than that. The work-family-work hierarchy is supported primarily by an ideology of marriage which emphasises the concept of partnership, a co-operative alliance of two individuals, each with distinctive and different things to offer, who engage in joint enterprises 'as a team' (Spedding, 1975, pp. 292–9). This partnership ideology of marriage, it will be argued in the next chapter, forms an important part of the way in which wives make sense of their incorporation in their husbands' work, and provides a powerful legitimation for that incorporation. For the moment, the discussion will concentrate on elaborating the *content* of that ideology.

The idea of marriage as partnership has come to be, as it were, the official morality of marriage, in place of the cruder official morality which emphasised a wife's subjection. Gray's (1977) discussion of the concept of matrimonial partnership in English law indicates that the 1882 Married Women's Property Act 'contains a rudimentary notion of sexual equality' (ibid., p. 50), but the concept of partnership was fully introduced in the Law Commission's report on family law in 1969, and its embodiment in the Matrimonial Proceedings and Property Act 1970 (ibid., p. 53). Its introduction was clearly intended as a replacement for the notion of the subordination of women: 'The incorporation in the law of the notion of partnership will achieve effective recognition of the fact that the wife is not an abject dependant of her husband, but is his equal in the enterprise of marriage' (ibid., p. 25). The notion of the marriage relationship captured by the concept of partnership is, according to Gray, 'that unique community of life and purpose which characterises the ideal relation of husband and wife. The enduring association of a man and a woman should be marked by a sharing of fortune and adversity, by love and constructive co-operation, by commitment, compromise and reciprocation' (ibid., pp. 23–4).

Although its embodiment in law may be of relatively recent origin, the concept of marriage as a partnership has a longer history, and has long been promoted by institutionalised religion. In the preface to the form for the solemnisation of matrimony in the Prayer Book of 1662, one of the three 'causes for which matrimony was ordained' is said to be 'for the mutual society, help and comfort that the one ought to have of the other, both in prosperity and in adversity' (Book of Common Prayer, 1662). Its appearance in the Prayer Book in this form should alert us to the fact that it is not always and necessarily an *alternative* to, or a replacement for, a concept of marriage which emphasises the subordination of wives, since in the same marriage services wives are required to promise to obey their husbands. It was, and still is, possible to hold together the two notions of a wife's position within the same ideology of marriage, and this is done through a partnership concept of marriage which implicitly assumes that the husband will be the *senior partner*. Thus, although at one level, contemporary family law treats marriage as a partnership, on another level 'for many legal and administrative purposes, husband and wife continue to be treated as a unit headed by the husband' (O'Donovan, 1979, p. 136). Cultural notions about a husband as senior partner are still reinforced by the operation of the legal system. Thus the partnership ideology of marriage has the effect of glossing over the relationships of domination and subordination between spouses, and of reconstituting them in a form which preserves the inherent power differential even if wives are accorded somewhat more protection than they previously enjoyed.

From the point of view of a wife's incorporation in her husband's work, the partnership ideology is important because it legitimates a wife's status as a junior partner, the 'helpmeet' (see above, Chapter 8). In so far as the notion of the helpmeet is still widely socially approved, it provides a strong justification for a wife's unpaid contributions to her husband's work, by transforming the performance of unpaid labour into a demonstration of being a *good wife*. As Papanek observes, 'The "two-person career" pattern is fully congruent with the stereotype of wife as supporter, comforter, backstage manager, home maintainer and rearer of children' (Papanek, 1973; p. 853).

Opportunities for women to be active helpmeets, or even to operationalise other aspects of marital partnership, are not evenly distributed among the population. There is a sense in which the notion of partnership is very much part of bourgeois ideology, which many working class women have little opportunity actively to share (Barrett, 1980, p. 204). But in so far as it is the part of an ideology which is promoted through legal, administrative and religious institutions, it forms (at the very least) an important context within which all wives have to make sense of their own marriages. The ways in which this operates will be discussed further in the next chapter.

Conclusion: the Three Jobs Syndrome

It is clear that wives' incorporation in a large measure depends upon the social and economic relations of contemporary marriage, which produce wives who are willing, and even eager, to be incorporated into their husbands' work. Recent work on the sociology of marriage, especially work informed by feminist perspectives, has begun to untangle the foundations and the expression of these relations. Some writers have focused upon the economic base of power within marriage (for example, Gillespie, 1972), while others have given equal emphasis to ideological conditions, especially the notion of patriarchy (for example, Kuhn, 1978). Others have concentrated upon the social forms which give expression to marriage relations: for example, Bell and Newby's (1976) discussion on the deferential dialectic between husbands and wives. This is not the place to do justice to these debates; but from them it is clear that, within contemporary marriages, most wives remain the junior partner and are kept in that position by the economic base of marriage, by prevailing ideologies and by cultural forms which give them expression.

Keeping a wife as the junior partner is central to maintaining the work-family-work hierarchy as the routine way in which the intersection between work–family and sexual divisions is handled on a day-to-day basis. Although it is clearly possible to envisage deviation from this model, the obstacles to sustaining alternative models are formidable, involving not only the practical logistics of, for example, handling child care when both parents are in full-time employment, but also overturning cultural images of appropriate relations between husband and wife. It is hardly surprising, therefore, that the conventional hierarchy of priorities remains the norm in most marriages. Once this hierarchy is accepted, the structuring of a wife's life by her husband's work, and the contributions which she makes to that work, flow naturally from it.

One consequence for wives who do undertake paid work is that they are probably faced not only with demonstrating that their children do not suffer as a result, but that their *husbands' work* does not suffer either. The clergymen's wives in my study certainly felt under a strong obligation to show this: although very few of them did any paid work, and only a handful worked full-time, those who did were at least as active as full-time housewives in supporting church activities and other aspects of their husbands' work. Wives who did not work were often quite explicit that they could only justify doing so if their husbands' work did not suffer as a consequence (Spedding, 1975, pp. 219–20). Similar sentiments are expressed about the wives of politicians by Mary Wilson, reviewing McLeod's (1976) book on the wives of Downing Street: 'Today's cabinet wives, *although supporting and encouraging their husbands* have, in most cases, their own work, often full-time professional work' (Wilson, 1976, p. 212) (my italics).

In practice, this means that there is a good chance that the employed wife will end up doing *three jobs*. Many others have noted that since employed women continue with their domestic and family work, they effectively do two jobs. I would argue that the labour which a wife contributes to her husband's work needs to be added to this, since it seems not to diminish significantly when wives are in paid employment themselves. Of course the nature and degree of contributions to a husband's work varies with the nature and organisation of that work, but where that contribution is more intensive, the three jobs syndrome is particularly apparent.

14

Making Sense of Being Married to the Job: Wives' Careers and Projects

In previous chapters it has been argued that the structural location and the cultural designation of a wife provide strong supports for a particular hierarchy of priorities, and considerable obstacles to the development of alternatives. To imply simply that wives have little choice but to accept this scheme of priorities, leaving them with little room for manoeuvre either practically or ideologically, would be to offer an excessively alienated and passive model of women merely on the receiving end of a system which they are powerless to change. It has already been suggested that the patterns of incorporation by and into one's husband's work *make sense* to many wives. This chapter will explore that claim more fully, looking at the patterns of incorporation from the wife's own perspective, and taking what would broadly be characterised as an interactionist perspective, in which wives are seen as active participants in shaping their own lives in meaningful ways within particular structural and cultural contexts.

This involves posing several linked questions. Why is it that wives continue to participate in these processes, despite the constraints which are placed upon them as a result, and despite the incorporation of their labour power for no payment? What are the benefits as well as the losses? Why do these processes appear 'natural' and unproblematic?

One answer which can be rejected straight away as an insufficient total explanation is the notion of socialisation. That is not to deny that the childhood experiences of women help to prepare them to accept subordinate positions in adult life, but the over-socialised conception of woman – to adapt Wrong's (1961) phrase – is too crude an account in itself precisely because it leaves no room at all for a woman as an independent actor, and at worst implies that women are too stupid to recognise what is being done to them. Past experiences constitute part – but only a part – of the material with which wives can work as they shape their lives in ways which make sense to them. To concentrate on material provided by the past neglects material provided in the present. Nor are wives straightforwardly socialised into accepting their incorporation, as if they were simply passive objects. That was very clear from my study of a small group of wives whose husbands were in training for the Church of England ministry. Despite the fact that they had been through the experience of residential training with their husbands, there was no evidence that their two or three years in theological college was responsible for making them into clergy wives, certainly not in any simple way. Rather it made much more sense to see it, in most cases, as a period of temporary flirtation with more radical ideas, before adopting more conventional modes of relating to their husbands' work once he was ordained (Spedding, 1975, p. 453).

The rest of this chapter attempts to elaborate the reasons why it makes sense for wives to be willing to be incorporated in their husbands' work, relating this discussion to issues about the structure and dynamics of marriage, which others have explored in different contexts. In turn, the consideration of the processes of incorporation provides a test of some of the analytical frameworks which others have developed. Finally, two conceptual models – careers and projects – are suggested as useful frameworks for understanding how wives do make sense of being married to the job.

Opting In

There are two main reasons why women continue to opt into being incorporated in their husbands' work (or perhaps one should say, continue to co-operate with the processes of incorporation, to remove any implication that the choice is totally free). First, there is a lack of viable alternatives; and secondly, there is the prospect that real benefits will be derived thereby. These issues of course are bound up with more general ones about why women continue to *marry* in such large numbers – and even to remarry after one unsatisfactory experience. However, it is clear that once married, it becomes fairly difficult to avoid the consequences of the work of the particular husband whom one has acquired.

The argument that a woman opts into marriage, and then into vicarious incorporation into her husband's work, because of the lack of viable alternatives, needs little further elaboration in the light of the analysis and evidence already presented. Marriage is the lifestyle which is structurally and culturally sustained and socially approved for women, and there is no comparable alternative pattern. Perhaps most compelling of all, marriage is the most economically viable option for most women, because a higher standard of living can be gained over a lifetime by being a wife than most women could achieve in their own right. In those circumstances it may well seem the most sensible economic option for a wife to invest her energies in her husband's work, thus promoting his earning potential, rather than to pursue her own.

Thus it seems that women do not only opt into the conventional pattern because they cannot envisage other options, but because it offers them positive economic benefits – although it must be acknowledged that such benefits can only be gained within the overall context of dependency. Other kinds of benefits also can derive from investment in one's husband's work. The notion that a wife will derive intrinsic personal satisfaction from supporting her husband's work – that is, from being a helpmeet – accords with the experience of some wives. Harris has characterised the contemporary family as one in which husband or wife (or both) may increasingly attempt to satisfy their creative energies within the context of the family, because they are denied expression elsewhere. This increased concentration of creative energies he characterises as 'implosion' – the metaphorical bursting inwards of the tensions so created (Harris, 1977, p. 79). If Harris is correct, it may be that a wife, denied real creative expression in the public domain in her own right, and left with only the family upon which to work, will actually be able to use her participation in her husband's work as a very real outlet for her creative energies (or perhaps one should say, whatever creative energies she has left after servicing her husband and children). To say that some women do find intrinsic satisfaction from being involved in their husbands' work is not to collude with the mystification of such participation which deems it as intrinsically satisfying, whatever the circumstances. Rather it is to recognise that, since wives are denied full (and often partial) participation in many sources of potential satisfaction available to men, the opportunity to engage in the public domain via their husbands' work may serve to expand their otherwise very limited opportunities.

Certain women very clearly can achieve higher social status vicariously than they could in their own right. This of course is true routinely in terms of wives' placing in the conventional social class hierarchy, because of the custom that women marry a man of higher status than themselves and take on his status ranking. But there is an additional dimension where one's husband's work is high status, where he is a public figure, a famous individual, or is accorded high prestige for whatever reason. In those circumstances, a woman's vicarious incorporation into her husband's work offers her immeasurably greater opportunities for high status and prestige than she would otherwise obtain. The according of equivalent diplomatic privileges to the wives of diplomats is one good illustration of this, and presumably wives of successful politicians commonly are accorded greater prestige than most would have acquired in any other way. To cite a totally untypical example, a journalist has described an interview with Nancy Reagan: ' "Why my joy is being Mrs. Ronald Reagan". Does she ever see herself as a separate person? "No, I never do. Always as Nancy Reagan." She continues, "My life *began* with Ronnie" ' (McPherson, 1975, p. 49) (italics original). Presumably investing one's whole persona in one's husband can be considered to have paid off if he ends up as President of the United States. But the idea of the trade-off is applicable more widely than simply to the wives of famous men: any example of a wife being partially absorbed into her husband's privileges, or basking in the reflected glory (however pale), is an example of her investment in him being repaid.

So there are real benefits as well as losses to be derived from incorporation into one's husband's work. That is not to suggest that wives make explicit benefit-and-loss calculations before or during marriage, still less that the notion of that kind of accounting would provide an adequate sociological account of the process of a wife's incorporation. But the recognition that there *are* benefits to be derived, albeit within an overall context which imposes considerable constraints upon women, begins to make it understandable that wives continue to opt in. They opt in not simply for lack of alternative, but because of the prospect of real gains.

Naturalness

There are good reasons why women continue to opt both into the processes of incorporation and into marriage. That opting in is made easy because it appears inherently natural to most people. There is of course a sense in which the whole of family life is constituted ideologically as part of a natural order, in which women are held to have a special place. Morgan has argued that sociologists reinforce these notions when they use concepts like 'family life cycle'. 'Family is said . . . to consist of an orderly sequence of events which are understood as the cultural realisation of the natural order. It is clear that the effective linking of family processes with a natural order is much clearer in the case of women than with men' (Morgan, 1975, pp. 183–4). Why does the particular case of incorporation into one's husband's work appear inherently natural?

First, and perhaps somewhat paradoxically, the fact that there is apparently some element of choice about whether to opt in makes the pattern appear more natural to those individuals who are in it than it would perhaps appear if it was actually imposed upon them, say with legal sanctions attached. This paradox is captured perfectly in the report on army welfare, which describes the role of the commanding officer's wife as one in which she 'traditionally and voluntarily' supports her husband (Ministry of Defence, 1976, para. 56). On the one hand, the claim that the support is 'voluntary' must be seriously undermined by the recognition that it is given 'traditionally', with all the military's structural and cultural supports for that tradition. On the other hand, precisely *because* the custom, whilst traditional, is not obligatory nor subject to formal sanctions, it can be seen as personal choice, therefore not imposed from outside, and therefore more likely to elicit a wife's personal identification if she 'chooses' it.

If a woman can envisage that it *could* be otherwise, but that she has chosen this pattern of her own volition, it makes it possible to believe that *in her own case* it is quite 'natural' for her to be the junior partner and to put her energies into supporting her husband's work. She can believe that she does it because her own talents and inclinations are suited to these arrangements – the fact that they also are the conventional arrangements is purely incidental. This kind of reasoning was common among the clergy wives in my study. Although very many of them were supporting their husbands' work in precisely those ways which the stereotype of the clergyman's wife would lead one to expect (such as attending women's groups and running activities for children), they often said that they did this not because it was expected of the clergyman's wife, but because they happened to enjoy doing that kind of thing. The very telling phrase that this is 'right for me' was commonly used (Spedding, 1975, ch. 11).

Secondly, patterns of incorporation appear quite natural because they are in step with other features of the marriage relationship. Whilst much of the literature on power relationships in marriage gives insufficient consideration to the way sexual divisions in marriage are structured, one feature of marriage which commonly emerges is that, in marital power games, wives most often give way, because husbands hold the balance of power despite the fact that the family is supposed to be the wife's domain (Gillespie, 1972, p. 126). Explanations of the operation of power relationships in marriage often ignore structurally generated inequities between husband and wife (Eichler, 1981), or operate entirely in the realm of ideas, treating normative prescriptions about appropriate actions for husband and wife as if they themselves constituted an explanation. An adequate explanation clearly has to integrate beliefs and structure. One useful example of such an explanation is Bell and Newby's notion of marriage as a relationship of deference, a form which is traditionally legitimated and ensures, not only that wives accept that their husbands *do* hold the greater power, but also that they *ought* to (Bell and Newby, 1976, p. 154).

This kind of analysis of the marriage relationship suggests that the established form of relationship is one in which the husband's needs and interests prevail and are accorded the greater priority. Thus the specific processes of incorporation into one's husband's work can be neatly integrated with this overall pattern.

Thirdly, this incorporation seems natural because the processes which it involves are concealed by the ideological separation of work and family. The ideological constitution of work and family as separate spheres, and of the separation of the public and the private domains, very effectively masks the contributions which women make. This happens because women are relegated to the private domain, and especially to the family, where their activities are less visible, and where they are defined out of the 'public work of production' (Stacey, 1981, pp. 172–3). Feminists who opened up the domestic labour debate were importantly responsible for demonstrating how women's 'private' activity in the home contributed vitally to social and ideological reproduction of capitalism. In a parallel way, the presumed separation of the two spheres powerfully conceals the fact that wives do contribute very significantly to economic production, via the labour which they invest both directly and indirectly in their husband's work. That relationship is concealed precisely because the home and family relationships are constituted ideologically as separate from production. Thus a wife's activity is seen as supporting *her husband* and investing *in him*, not as labour gratuitously offered to his employer. It is seen rather as a natural feature of the marriage relationship.

The corollary is that failure to support one's husband's work is quite likely to be interpreted as a sign that the health of the marriage is suspect. Indeed, there is a sense in which declining to support his work does of itself constitute marriage 'failure' since it is an explicit sign that a wife is rejecting the helpmeet role, and therefore not really acting as a wife. The empirical material from the clergymen's wives' study suggests a strong identification between helping one's husband's work and having a good marriage (see above, Chapter 9 for further discussion), perhaps best encapsulated in the comment, 'I don't see how you couldn't become involved if you were complete in your marriage' (Spedding, 1975, p. 256).

Fourthly, the processes of incorporation are powerfully legitimated through very public displays of the partnership ideology in operation, in contexts where wives are seen clearly to derive satisfaction and other benefits from supporting their husbands. It is for this reason that well-publicised instances of politicians' wives, for example, standing by their husbands on the platform and sharing closely in their victory, cannot simply be dismissed as atypical examples, not relevant to the average wife. Similarly, Lady Diana Spencer's comment, in a television interview on the eve of her marriage to the Prince of Wales, that she looked forward to being a good wife (*Guardian*, 28 July 1981) provided a very public example of partnership ideology in action. Conspicuous public examples of the supportive wife of course provide opportunities for atypical forms of incorporation precisely because they are very public, but the image of the supportive wife is by no means confined to these situations. Indeed, there is a sense in which the 'partnership' of all wives is legitimated by those who demonstrate their support for men who do 'worthwhile' jobs (like the clergy) or 'important' jobs (like politicians and royalty). These women are engaging in activities which are socially approved *for a wife*; and if their 'helpmeet' activities are more visible than most, they may simply be regarded as especially fortunate in having the opportunity of demonstrating their partnership publicly. In this way, the incorporation of a wife's labour, which in other circumstances might be interpreted as exploitation, can be constituted as a *privilege*. That certainly was the case for the clergymen's wives in my study, who regarded their support for their husbands' work not as a specific consequence of being married to a clergyman, but as the outworking, in a particular setting, of being a good wife (Spedding, 1975, pp. 245–57).

Thus women who work through the helpmeet role in very auspicious and very public settings serve as models for other wives, and provide a clear demonstration of the possible advantages of investing in a husband. They provide models to which other women can aspire precisely because it is recognisably *wifely* activities which they undertake. Thus Mary Wilson's description of the 'ideal' of a Prime Minister's wife specifies elements in that ideal which are capable of translation into much humbler settings. All the wives described in McLeod's (1977) book are, she writes,

> alike in one thing – dedication to their husbands as prime ministers. Then, as now, the role of the prime minister's wife was a supporting one. Many people have an idea of the perfect prime minister's wife – a woman totally committed to her husband's ideals, politically aware, a perfect hostess, tactful, diplomatic, serenely bending others to her will while remaining completely poised and charming. Each of the women in the book seemed to be trying, in her own way, to achieve this ideal.   (Wilson, 1976, p. 212)

Apart from the item of political awareness, the themes are so familiar: support, commitment, tact, diplomacy, poise and being a good hostess. Even Prime Ministers' wives are variations on the same helpmeet theme.

Finally, incorporation into one's husband's work seems natural because to go along with it provides a framework for daily life which, whilst it may have some unwelcome features, at least is structured and ordered. Moreover, the order is framed so as to be entirely understandable to other people – it is culturally a highly accessible context. This means that it provides a framework through which to conduct routine interactions in a relatively unproblematic way. Conversely, women who do not conduct routine interactions in this way are by definition constituted as deviants, whose actions threaten the 'natural' order: in such circumstances, 'most people do not think to deviate' (Stacey and Price, 1980, p. 34). To give a very simple example: precisely *because* a woman's social status is commonly defined by her husband's, routine contacts with public agencies often proceed on the basis of the presumed need for information about one's husband's job. Macintyre's study of note-taking in an antenatal clinic documents the anxiety generated when information about the occupation of a patient's husband is not available (Macintyre, 1978, p. 595). Faced with the choice of simply giving the information requested, or refusing on grounds of independence from one's husband, it is always easier to give the information, since the interaction is likely to proceed in a much less problematic fashion thereafter.

In the next section, it will be argued that the kind of orderliness imposed by accepting the processes of incorporation into one's husband's work can best be understood as a vicarious career.

Vicarious Careers

The analogy of the career, it will be argued, offers a useful conceptual framework for analysing the ways in which wives make sense of their own lives in relation to their husbands'; that is, their lives are lived as a 'wife of' career, parallel to his, and tied to it at every point. This is not to say that wives explicitly recognise this vicarious career pattern, although some do. Some wives invest so much of their energy and of themselves in participation in their husbands' work that it becomes explicitly a joint enterprise. In her historical work on army wives, for example, Bamfield describes how wives referred to 'our' or even 'my' regiment, and encouraged their daughters to marry within it (Bamfield, 1975, p. 16); and in my study of clergymen's wives, it was not uncommon to find them referring to 'our appointment' or 'our parish'. Fowlkes reports that American doctors' wives commonly speak of 'our practice' (Fowlkes, 1980, p. 70). This identification of some individual wives may be very strong indeed. Dora Russell, writing of the ending of her marriage to Bertrand Russell, says, 'This was more than a marriage, it had seemed like a professional career. What should I do now that I had, so to speak, lost my job?' (Russell, 1980, p. 3).

The use of the word 'career' here needs some clarification. In the interactionist tradition at least (Fowlkes, 1980, p. 1), the concept of career need not apply only to paid work. Everett Hughes has argued that the concept of career is by no means confined to paid work because 'there are other points at which one's life touches the social order' (Hughes, 1958, p. 64), and he explicitly acknowledges that a woman may have a career in the context of the family. His concept of career essentially is that it is a perspective for conceptualising the meaning of social life. 'Subjectively, a career is the moving perspective through which a person sees his life as a whole and interprets the meaning of his various attributes, actions and the things which happen to him' (ibid., p. 63).

Other writers have used the concept of career with reference to wives, but not exactly in the way which I intend. Papanek's discussion of the 'two-person career' is very close to my usage, but she confines her analysis to the wives of men in professional and executive work (see above, Chapter 1). It has already been demonstrated that the processes of incorporation into one's husband's work apply much more widely. Nevertheless, Papanek's conceptualisation is important, because it identifies the possibility that an occupational career can *include* a wife, who participates in it without being formally acknowledged and without being directly remunerated.

The other writer who has made very interesting use of the concept of career in relation to wives is Kate Purcell. Her usage is somewhat different, since she directs our attention to marriage itself *as* the career of a woman (Purcell, 1978). She argues in fact that 'being a woman is itself seen in career terms', and that both boys and girls are brought up to regard a 'woman's main career as a wife to a breadwinning male and the mother of his children' (ibid., p. 154). I wish to argue that, within this overall career of being a woman, one can identify the specific strand of a 'wife of' career, that is, of vicarious incorporation into one's husband's occupation, and that this constitutes a very clear application of the career analogy of wives. Purcell acknowledges that separate strands can be identified in this way: 'Whilst motherhood and the housewife role may be seen as jobs or careers in themselves, they are in fact parts, sometimes stages, of the career of being a woman' (ibid., p. 155).

My usage of the term 'career' denotes a woman's incorporation into her husband's work in a patterned way, which parallels his own experience of that work, within the overall context of her career as a woman. To have a vicarious 'career', a woman does not have to be married to a man who works in a hierarchical or bureaucratic setting, or in a professional job, although the parallels will be more explicit when they are tied to this type of work. The form of 'wife of' careers will vary, but in so far as any man's work provides him with some kind of organising theme for his wife (even if it is seen more clearly retrospectively), his wife can make sense and order of her life in relation to that theme.

In drawing on the concept of career in the interactionist tradition, one is focusing upon what Goffman has called 'an exercise in the institutional approach to the study of the self' (Goffman, 1968, p. 119). In this tradition, a career is an observable pattern, linked to an individual's social location and changes in that location, but it is also a linked series of changes in the interior of that individual's life. 'A frame of reference for studying careers is, at the same time, a frame for studying personal identities. . . central to any account of adult identity is the relation of change in identity to change in social position' (Strauss and Becker, 1975, p. 95). The concept of career is especially useful in relation to wives' incorporation in their husbands' work, because it crosses the false divide between the public and the private, and directs our attention to tracing the links between the two. Papanek recognises this in her discussion of the two-person career:

> The specific topic of this discussion – 'vicarious achievement' in the two-person single career – is concerned with the transactions which occur at the boundary between public and private spheres. They involve a three-way relationship between employers and two partners in a marriage, in which two sets of relationships are of the 'secondary' type and one is of the 'primary'.
>
> (Papanek, 1973, p. 855)

A career, in this perspective, is an orderly way of making sense of one's life in a specific social setting, and it sets a framework for interaction to which others can relate. As Hughes says, writing of male occupational careers, 'Institutions are but the forms in which the collective behaviour and collective action of people go on. In the course of a career the person finds his place within these forms, carries on his active life with reference to other people, and interprets the meaning of the one life he has to live' (Hughes, 1958, p. 67).

How does this apply to the incorporation of wives in their husbands' work? Vicarious, 'wife of' careers can be analysed within the framework set down by Goffman, in probably what is the best application of the concept of career to a non-work setting: his discussion of the moral career of the mental patient. He gives a fourfold definition of what constitutes a career: any social strand of a person's course through life; changes over time which can be seen as basic and common to members of a given social category; on the one hand, the strand identified is seen by the individual as part of their own self-image and felt identity; on the other hand, it is part of a publicly accessible institutional context (Goffman, 1968, p. 119). It can readily be seen how career, defined in this sense, can apply to situations much wider than paid work, and this fourfold definition helps to draw out many features of vicarious, 'wife of' careers.

First, the 'wife of' career – being a policeman's wife, an oilman's wife, or whatever – forms a consistent strand through many women's lives. This is not to say that such consistency cannot be disrupted, nor certainly that the strand is always orderly and predictable. The experience of orderliness, whilst sometimes implied by the concept of career, is not the experience of many male workers in their occupational careers (Wilensky, 1961), nor is the notion of predictability necessary to this model of the career: 'the career of any individual cannot be known at any point ahead of time; careers are always *lived* and the future remains unknown . . . a career as experienced *unfolds*; it is not viewed as a whole by the individual until it is over' (Krause, 1971, pp. 44–5). Nor does it necessarily imply *upward* progression: 'careers have direction – up, down and sideways' (ibid., p. 43). The key features of the career are, in Krause's view, pattern and experience (ibid., p. 42). As 'wife of' careers are lived and experienced, the pattern unfolds, to be understood most fully in retrospect, just like the male occupational careers to which they are tied.

The consistency of the vicarious career strand in a wife's life derives from the ways in which features of her husband's work so significantly structure her life: his work is always there, to be accommodated, responded to and assisted. There are circumstances in which his work forms a more consistent strand for her than it does for him: if a male worker moves to a different firm, for example, he may experience this as a considerable disruption in the relationship between his work and his personal identity; but to his wife, the patterning which his work imposes upon her, and other demands which it makes, may remain essentially the same.

One event with major potential for disrupting the consistency of the vicarious career is of course the ending of the marriage. That possibility does not, however, totally undermine the argument that 'wife of' careers form a major consistent strand through many women's lives, for three reasons. First, even if the vicarious career does end with separation or divorce, it is likely still to have lasted longer, and to have been more consistent while it did last, than any 'career' which a wife has in adult life related to her own employment. Secondly, since many divorced women do remarry, they may actually experience only a temporary break in their 'wife of' career, even if it takes a somewhat different shape the second time around: in this context, divorce and remarriage seem more or less the equivalent of changing jobs. Thirdly, for many women divorce is not a total break. This point is brought out very cogently by Delphy, writing from within a very different tradition, when she argues that the appropriation of a wife's labour continues after divorce in most cases, because usually women take on the total day-to-day care of the children, with very low financial input from the man. Thus the 'collective exploitation' of women by men continues (Delphy, 1976, pp. 86–7), and 'divorce is not the opposite of marriage, nor even its end, but simply a change or transformation of marriage' (ibid., p. 82) In terms of the 'wife of' career, divorce can be a modification of it, rather than its removal. Certainly divorce does not necessarily remove the constraints of the former husband's work: his earning capacity will still be the major determinant of his ex-wife's living standards in many cases; and his pattern of continuing contact with his children will be structured by his working patterns, which his former wife will have to continue to accommodate. The extent to which a former wife derives aspects of her personal identity from her husband's work is less clear, and there is some interesting empirical work to be done here: what is the social meaning of being a 'former wife of' a particular individual? One can certainly think of examples where former wives of prestigious and famous men continue to be accorded a certain amount of status and prestige as a result – although probably a reduced amount by comparison with the woman who continues as a wife. On the other hand, being a 'former wife of' also must constitute in some degree a spoiled identity, from which one would expect more negative consequences to ensue (Goffman, 1963).

Secondly, Goffman defines a career as consisting of changes over time which can be seen as basic and common to members of a given social category. This certainly is applicable to 'wife of' careers. It has been a basic theme of this study that certain experiences are common to, and shared by, wives of men in particular occupational settings. As a man proceeds through various changes over time in his working situation, his wife experiences parallel changes, which structure her own life. Certain of these changes are unavoidable: changes in the organisation of his work, which inevitably change the patterns imposed on her own life, and the way in which she is treated by others. This can happen whatever the direction of the change: the alteration in patterning of her life or in her public identity is equally significant if the change is from 'teacher's wife' to 'headmaster's wife', as it is for the change from 'teacher's wife' to 'redundant teacher's wife' – although no doubt the former change is more welcome than the latter.

Although certain features of changes over time are unavoidable, because they are externally imposed, other kinds of changes linked to a husband's occupational changes require, as it were, a wife's co-operation. Goffman describes a moral career as 'a career laying out progressive changes in the beliefs [the individual] has concerning himself and significant others' (Goffman, 1961, p. 317). The moral career of being a 'wife of' entails changes in the beliefs which a wife has about herself and her husband, that is, changes in felt identity. The Colonel's Lady, writing in the *SAAFA Magazine*, gives a delightful illustration of what these changes meant to her when her husband was first promoted: 'I had yet to grow accustomed to the mantle of greatness which had descended upon me. To become a Colonel's Lady had never been among my ambitions in life . . . Yet in time the subaltern I married became a lieutenant colonel, and I – his lady. Such is fame' (*SAAFA Magazine, 1957–8,* p. 6). Changes in felt identity, and the production of appropriate social actions, are not automatic nor even always welcomed in the vicarious career, even if the movement is in an upward direction. This is well recognised by employers who, according to Papanek, sometimes relate a man's promotion prospects to the 'suitability' of his wife. 'The most important aspect of this suitability is related to social mobility, that is, whether a wife is able to maintain a certain kind of lifestyle, and to change along with her husband's changes in rank, but no faster or slower' (Papanek, 1973, p. 859). So wives can be judged according to their performance of this aspect of the vicarious career, that is, the extent to which they can 'keep up with' their husband, and their performance may be quite crucial to their husbands' prospects.

The third and fourth parts of Goffman's definition of a career are opposite sides of the same coin, and emphasise how the concept of career links the public and private domains: career as both felt identity, and publicly accessible context.

The centrality of work for a man's self-identity has been a common theme in sociological literature. For example Hughes, in an influential paper, wrote, 'a man's work is one of the more important aspects of his social identity, his self' (Hughes, 1958, p. 43). At the same time, it has often been suggested that the equivalent for women is the centrality of the family: 'Men . . . of course form personal attachments, and women work for a lifetime inside and outside the home. However, it remains true that the man's foothold in the work-a-day world is basic to his concept of masculine selfhood, and the woman's intimate relations with others are basic to her concept of feminine selfhood'

(Hunt, 1980, p. 7). An examination of the processes and consequences of a wife's incorporation in her husband's work suggests that the 'wife of' identity thereby conferred may provide a woman with a personal identity just as significant as any derived from intimate relationships, especially if she is a 'wife of' someone whose job is socially valued, respected, or prestigious. Indeed, in those circumstances, the vicarious occupational identity may appear an enticing prospect by comparison with the other identity which is available to her, that of 'housewife', which is hardly a very attractive alternative (Oakley, 1974a, pp. 184–7).

Being a 'wife of' an individual in a particular occupation clearly is *an* identity available to all wives. The circumstances in which it will become a *major* personal identity, or even take precedence over other available identities, is a more complex question, and clearly open to empirical investigation. In my study of clergymen's wives, it seemed that the 'clergy wife' identity was rated against other personal identities in a fairly complex way (Spedding, 1975, pp. 526–31). To argue that is not to imply a highly fragmented model of the self (Brittan, 1973, ch. 9) in which an individual is conceptualised as a bundle of identities, to be taken up and discarded at will; rather that a variety of fairly discrete identities are *available* to any individual. In the case of clergymen's wives, they seemed to handle this not by developing ways of integrating them hierarchically in order of importance, but by giving each one a weighting of importance and compatibility in relation to the others. Thus most claimed for themselves the identity of 'good wife and mother' and kept this separate from their 'clergy wife' identity, assigning the higher priority to the former. These two identities were seen as having quite a high degree of compatibility, whereas the identity of 'worker' was seen as being relatively incompatible with both, and was assigned a fairly low priority. On the other hand, it did seem possible for 'worker' to take precedence over 'clergy wife' if work was seen as strictly necessary for the family economy – that is, where it integrated well with 'good wife and mother' (Spedding, 1975, pp. 526–32).

This example from the clergymen's wives study serves to illustrate some of the complexities of handling the notion of 'wife of' identities, and of handling the relationship between identities and actions. However, the argument still holds that the vicarious occupational identity is not only a possible one, but an important one for many wives. It is important precisely because it is one available identity which does not confine a woman to the private, domestic sphere, but which offers her some kind of foothold, albeit a vicarious one, in the public domain.

This brings us to Goffman's final characteristic of a career: that it is a publicly accessible context in which an individual can be located. 'Wife of' careers certainly provide this. The variety of ways in which wives become publicly identified with their husbands' work have already been illustrated, and that identification can sometimes take very concrete forms, as in the singularly unpleasant example of Irish girls marrying British soldiers stationed in Ulster, and being tarred and feathered as a result (*SAAFA Magazine*, January 1972, p. 2).

If 'wife of' is a public context, then the more 'public' a man's work, the more significant is that context likely to be for his wife: in some circumstances it may become the key context in which other people relate to her. That was certainly the case for the clergymen's wives in my study, who found it difficult to persuade others to relate to them as anything other than the minister's or vicar's wife, and wives of other 'public figures' seem to reflect similar experiences (see above, pp. 39–41). In this context, the practice of employers vetting wives makes a great deal of sense. Whom a man has for friends or even lovers is of comparatively little importance to his employer, but whom he has for a wife is of profound significance, since she will become identified with him and with his work in a unique way. Hence the commanders of the nineteenth-century British army were not disturbed by having groups of prostitutes following their troops around, but they had to be consulted before their officers could marry (Bamfield, 1975, pp. 13–20).

The career analogy has been used here as a conceptual tool with which to examine some of the ways in which incorporation into one's husband's work can offer a wife a framework within which to make sense of her own life, and within which to create orderliness. It is an attractive framework, because it offers a public context to which others can relate, and the possibility of a personal identity superior to some others which are accessible to wives. The character of what is offered varies of course with one's husband's occupation, and some 'wife of' identities are far more desirable than others.

Wives' Projects

The emphasis in this chapter has been not so much on the external structures and constraints through which wives are hedged in, but upon wives as active human beings, shaping their own lives and investing them with meaning. Those tasks take place within a context where the territory is, as it were, mapped out by social structures, and where commonly accepted cultural meanings provide materials with which individuals can work. The creative activity is on-going, not accomplished once and for all, and to that extent images of the future may be more important than images of the present for the way wives both think about and act upon their relationship to their husbands' work.

The concept of personal projects is one which offers a fruitful conceptualisation here, emphasising as it does an interpretative understanding of the actor, and the need to see individuals as oriented to the possibilities for the future, rather than simply tied to the opportunities of the present. In his discussion of personal projects, Morgan (1975, pp. 213–19) acknowledges that the concept derives from Sartre, and the emphasis is on individual human actors as attempting to construct a preferred present and future for themselves. Morgan suggests that the family might be understood in terms of the projects of its members, each of whom needs the others to some extent in order to realise personal projects, and who can either assist or hinder each other in their realisation. So the family can be examined in relation to the overlapping projects of its members, and in particular, 'the way in which these projects are realised or denied through the co-presence of others also seeking to realise their projects and the way in which projects become alienated, that is, take on a life of their own and appear to confront the agent as an alien object rather than as the agent's *own* project' (ibid., p. 216) (italics original).

As Morgan himself suggests, where an occupational career provides a central theme for a man, it will probably do so for his family as well. 'Thus the husband's project is realised with the aid of and through his wife; the wife's project is defined in terms of her husband. This reminds us that, while at one level one might say that all projects are equal at another level there is considerable inequality particularly with respect to the way that one actor is able to determine the project of the other' (ibid., p. 217).

One way of viewing the intersection between sexual divisions and work–family is to ask the question: how much space is left for a wife to develop *her* projects within the context of those two sets of social relations, and how far is she inevitably constrained to define her projects in relation to her husband's? In the construction of their own personal projects, most wives have little choice but to take account of their husbands' work. A possible and, it is suggested, a common response is to incorporate that work as part of the wife's own project. The way in which this seems to happen is that a wife makes on-going investments in her husband's work, and in doing so, becomes committed to continuing to do so.

The idea that wives invest time and energy in facilitating their husbands' work, and sometimes directly assisting in it, has already been well explored in this study. In my study of clergymen's wives, it became very clear that wives, to use Becker's phrase, had 'staked' things of value upon their husbands' work (Finch, 1980, p. 862). Becker sees this as part of the process whereby lines of action develop over time into commitments by making a series of 'side bets' (Becker, 1970, p. 44). In Becker's view, this process creates its own dynamic: once an individual has staked on a particular line of action (be it with money, reputation, or anything else of value to her) it becomes difficult to withdraw, because 'the consequences of inconsistency will be so expensive that inconsistency . . . is no longer a feasible alternative' (ibid.). The evidence reviewed in this study suggests that wives commonly do make those kind of investments in their husbands' work, and that once begun, it becomes difficult to withdraw because withdrawal would mean loss of potential future increased income and loss of face, to say nothing of possible loss of a husband. All of these apply with more force where the husband is climbing a career ladder, especially if the prospects look good. Moreover, in the very process of facilitating her husband's work, a wife is likely to have reduced her capacity for developing alternatives on her own. The process is very easily begun, since other alternatives may be also structurally blocked. 'The occupational system effectively excludes most women from high status jobs by saying that women have a higher emotional investment in the family – the more they are driven back on the family, the more they *will* develop such investments' (Gowler and Legge, 1978, p. 50) (italics original).

So men's work becomes incorporated in wives' projects through the investments which women make, but that does not necessarily mean that commitment to continue is an intended outcome, or even a forseen outcome. Krause, in an interesting discussion of the use of the concept of commitment in the work of Becker and of Kierkegaard, suggests that the philosopher's understanding of commitment emphasises conscious choice and intention, whereas 'for the sociologist Becker, a person is committed by what has happened to him, not what he has chosen' (Krause, 1971, p. 56). In this perspective, commitments develop through actions taken, but they may well be the unintended and unexpected consequences of those actions. 'Becker suggests that commitment to a career be defined as that point in the history of the career where more goods and rewards would be lost in leaving the career . . . than the conceivable or ascertainable rewards of trying a different career. The process may be partially *unwitting* and unintended, the person waking up to find himself committed' (ibid., p. 46) (italics original). It is suggested that wives' projects are precisely of that nature: because of actions taken over a period of time, many a wife must, as it were, wake up to find herself committed to the further promotion or facilitation of her husband's work, in order to realise other possible projects – such as improvement in her own standard of living, or that of her children, for example. Of course withdrawal is always *possible*, but the point of real commitment is reached when it becomes *too expensive* to contemplate seriously. The vicarious 'wife of' career can become a valuable commodity. A wife's failure to continue to support her husband's work means not only that she risks undermining his position, but also that she herself has something to lose. A corollary of this argument would be that a wife can stop investing in her husband when there is *nothing* to lose – when he is nearing retirement maybe. An empirical study which tested systematically whether wives feel more able to resist incorporation in their husbands' work once further investment seems unnecessary would be very interesting indeed.

The opportunity for a wife to make investments in her husband's work must be related to some extent to the character and organisation of that work. As was argued in relation to wives of men nearing retirement, it may be that some wives stop making investments (or never really begin) because they see no real prospect of further improving their husbands' position. Again, empirical studies which test out this issue across a range of occupations would make an important contribution. In their absence, one can only speculate that investments made vary with men's occupations in similar ways to other aspects of wives' incorporation. Thus, on one level, the value of making investments seems most obvious in professional and bureaucratic careers, and therefore the notion of investments suggests that wives' incorporation perhaps *is* significantly class-linked (see above, pp. 124–30). However, material discussed in this study would suggest that such a view needs to be modified to take account of other instances. Wives of self-employed electricians, for example, or of publicans whose income derives mainly from commission on goods sold, would seem to have equally valid reasons for expecting that investing in their husbands' work might be worthwhile. It is, in other words, not the particular job done, certainly not simply whether it 'counts' as manual or non-manual, which makes a wife's investments more or less worthwhile, but a combination of features related to the organisation of the work, arrangements for remuneration and the relations of production under which the male worker operates.

Finally, when wives include the facilitating of their husbands' work in their own projects, that carries within it a potential contradiction. If their investment pays off, they stand to make real gains, but those investments by their nature cannot be realised except in terms of *the husband's* activity. This particular project is one in which the participation of someone else is crucial, and there is no necessary guarantee that husband's and wife's projects will accord with each other in this respect: witness the cultural imagery about a wife who 'pushes her husband too hard'. Thus the promotion of one's husband's work provides a good example of Morgan's observation about family projects needing the co-presence of others seeking to realise their projects. It also illustrates his observation about one's own project taking on the character of an alien object. Once commitments have developed to the point where it seems too expensive to withdraw, a wife may feel that she has no choice but to go on. This is the point at which, as it were, the creature which she created by her own actions becomes a creature which makes demands which must be met, and whose controls cannot be avoided. Certainly many clergy wives saw the demands associated with their husbands' work as demands which could not be avoided, although it seemed to me that these were precisely demands arising from commitments which they themselves had developed over time (Finch, 1980, p. 862; Spedding, 1975, pp. 454–60). Further work on the incorporation of wives in their husbands' work could usefully document these processes for other occupational groups.

Concluding Remarks

Being married to the job makes perfect sense for most wives, not simply because external constraints force them into it, nor because their socialisation makes their compliance inevitable, but because it has its own inherent internal logic. This internal logic has three strands: it makes economic good sense; the organisation of social life makes compliance easy and developing alternatives very difficult; it provides a comprehensible way of being a wife.

First, whether or not marriage is unequivocally the best economic option for most women, once in a marriage, it usually makes economic sense to stay in it and to invest in one's husband. It makes sense because, once married, the chance of developing an independent economic base equal or superior to one's husband is remote. So most wives' best economic option is to invest what they can in their husbands' work, in the hope of improving his position, and thereby their own. The converse of this argument is that if a woman does develop a strong alternative economic base, part of the internal logic of being married to the job – indeed of being married – is removed. As Turner (1971) has argued, the dissolution of marriage between dual-career couples is more *likely* precisely because it is more *possible*.

Secondly, social life is organised on the assumption that most wives *are* married to the job. Illustrations of this range from those which affect everyone (like the lack of publicly provided child care facilities because it is assumed that most children have full-time mothers releasing men for full-time work), to situations which are very much minority experiences (the expectation that the wives of home-based workers will organise the home around his needs, for example). The effect of social life being organised on the assumption that wives *will* be married to the job is that compliance is made easy, and rejection very difficult. The wife who wishes *not* to be married to the job becomes the deviant, is placed on the defensive and has to justify herself, and will meet major obstacles in trying to organise her life so as to avoid incorporation. Faced with such daunting prospects, being married to the job is bound to seem the easier course of action, or indeed the only possible one.

Thirdly, being married to the job smooths routine social interactions because it provides a comprehensible way of being a good wife, indeed of being a wife. Like the second strand of the internal logic, it may come to seem like the only way in which it is possible to handle daily life. I have argued elsewhere that wives of the clergy rapidly revert to the conventional model of the clergyman's wife (even if they begin in other ways) precisely because that offers an *understandable* performance (Spedding, 1975, ch. 19). A parallel here is Voysey's argument that parents with a handicapped child, in making sense of their own situation, draw upon the official morality of the 'normal family' and adapt it to their own circumstances precisely because that provides a basis upon which interactions with others at least become possible (Voysey, 1975, especially ch. 8). So too, wives need to be able to use publicly accessible, and therefore commonly understood, cultural and linguistic forms in order to be able to conduct social interactions *as wives*. Refusal to be married to the job so seriously challenges the partnership model of marriage that it is difficult to contain it within a comprehensible public performance as a wife.

Add to this internal logic the internal dynamic that, once one has begun on the path of incorporation, one tends to become committed to continuing, and there are the ingredients which explain why it makes perfect sense for a wife (at least so long as she wishes to remain a wife) to be – and to continue to be – married to the job.

Bibliography

Abrams, P. and McCulloch, A. (1976), 'Men, women and communes', in *Sexual Divisions and Society: Process and Change* (London: Tavistock), pp. 246–75.

Acker, J. (1973), 'Women and social stratification: a case of intellectual sexism', *American Journal of Sociology*, vol. 78, no. 4, pp. 936–45.

Allan, G. (1979), *A Sociology of Friendship and Kinship* (London: Allen & Unwin).

Bailyn, L. (1978), 'Accommodation of work to family', in *Working Couples,* ed. R. Rapoport and R. N. Rapoport (London: Routledge & Kegan Paul).

Baker, J. C. (1976), 'Company policies and executives' wives abroad', *Industrial Relations*, vol. 15, no. 3, pp. 343–8.

Bamfield, V. (1975), *On the Strength: The British Army Wife* (London: Knight).

Banton, M. (1964), *The Policeman in the Community* (London: Tavistock).

Barker, D. L. (1977), 'The regulation of marriage: repressive benevolence', in *Power and the State*, ed. G. Littlejohn, B. Smart, J. Wakeford and N. Yuval-Davis (London: Croom Helm), pp. 239–66.

Barker, D. L. and Allen, S. (1976a), *Dependence and Exploitation in Work and Marriage* (London: Longman).

Barker, D. L. and Allen, S. (1976b), *Sexual Divisions and Society: Process and Change* (London: Tavistock).

Barrett, M. (1980), *Women's Oppression Today: Problems in Marxist Feminist Analysis* (London: Verso).

Barrett, M. and McIntosh, M. (1979), 'Christine Delphy: towards a materialist feminism?', *Feminist Review*, no. 1, pp. 96–106.

Bechhofer, F., Elliott, B., Rushforth, M. and Bland, R. (1974a), 'The petit bourgeois in the class structure: the case of small shopkeepers', in *The Social Analysis of Class Structure*, ed. F. Parkin (London: Tavistock), pp. 103–28.

Bechhofer, F., Elliott, B., Rushforth, M. and Bland, R. (1974b), 'Small shopkeepers: matters of money and meaning', *Sociological Review*, vol. 22, pp. 465–80.

Becker, H. (1970), *Sociological Work* (Chicago: Aldine).

Becker, H. S. (1971), 'The nature of a profession', in *Sociological Work*, ed. H. S. Becker (Harmondsworth: Penguin), pp. 87–103.

Beechey, V. (1977), 'Female wage labour in capitalist production', *Capital and Class*, no. 3, pp. 45–66.

Beechey, V. (1978), 'Critical analysis of some sociological theories of women's work', in *Feminism and Materialism*, ed. A. Kuhn and A. M. Wolpe (London: Routledge & Kegan Paul), pp. 155–97.

Beechey, V. (1979), 'On patriarchy', *Feminist Review*, no. 3, pp. 66–82.

Bell, C. (1968), *Middle Class Families* (London: Routledge & Kegan Paul).

Bell, C. and Newby, H. (1976), 'Husbands and wives: the dynamics of the deferential dialectic', in *Dependence and Exploitation in Work and Marriage*, ed. D. L. Barker and S. Allen (London: Longman), pp. 152–68.

Benham, L. (1974), 'Benefits of women's education within marriage', in

Economics of the Family, Marriage, Children and Human Capital, ed. T. W. Schultz (Chicago: University of Chicago Press).

Berger, M., Foster, M. and Wallston, B. S. (1978), 'Finding two jobs', in *Working Couples*, ed. R. Rapoport and R. N. Rapoport (London: Routledge & Kegan Paul), pp. 23–35.

Berk, R. A. and Berk, S. F. (1979), *Labour and Leisure at Home: Content and Organisation of the Household Day* (Beverly Hills, Calif.: Sage).

Bertaux, D. and Bertaux-Wiame, I. (1981), 'Artisanal bakery in France: how it lives and why it survives', in *The Petit Bourgeoisie: Comparative Studies of the Uneasy Stratum*, ed. F. Bechofer and B. Elliot (London: Macmillan), pp. 155–81.

Blackstone, T. and Fulton, O. (1975), 'Sex discrimination among university teachers: a British and American comparison', *British Journal of Sociology*, vol. 26, no. 3, pp. 261–75.

Blood, R. O. (1969), *Marriage*, 2nd edn (New York: Free Press).

Bott, E. (1957), *The Family and Social Network* (London: Tavistock).

Brezeskwinski, J. (1981), 'The geographical mobility of women in "dual career" households: determinants and consequences', Paper presented to the 77th Annual Meeting of the Association of American Geographers.

Brittan, A. (1973), *Meanings and Situations* (London: Routledge & Kegan Paul).

Bromley, P. M. (1976), *Family Law*, 5th edn (London: Butterworths).

Burke, G. (1981), *Housing and Social Justice* (London: Longman).

Burkitt, B. and Rose, M. (1981), 'Why be a wife?', *Social Review*, vol. 29, no. 1, pp. 67–76.

Burns, S. (1975), *The Household Economy* (Boston, Mass.: Beacon Press).

Cain, M. (1973), *Society and the Policeman's Role* (London: Routledge & Kegan Paul).

Callan, H. (1975), 'The premiss of dedication: notes towards an ethnography of diplomats' wives', in *Perceiving Women*, ed. S. Ardner (London: Mallaby), pp. 87–104.

Chamberlain, M. (1975), *Fenwomen: A Portrait of Women in an English Village* (London: Virago/Quartet Books).

Chisholm, L. A. (1977), 'The comparative career development of graduate women and men', *Women's Studies International Quarterly*, vol. 1, no. 4, pp. 327–40.

Chisholm, L. and Woodward, D. (1980), 'The experiences of women graduates in the labour market', in *Schooling for Women's Work*, ed. R. Deem (London: Routledge & Kegan Paul), pp. 162–76.

Church of England (1980), *Alternative Service Book* (London: Hodder & Stoughton).

Clark, D. (1982), *Between Pulpit and Pew: Folk religion in a North Yorkshire Fishing Village* (Cambridge: CUP).

Cohen, G. (1977), 'Absentee husbands in spiralist families', *Journal of Marriage and the Family*, vol. 39, pp. 595–604.

Comer, L. (1974), *Wedlocked Women* (Leeds: Feminist Books).

Comes, L. (1978), 'The question of women and class', *Women's Studies International Quarterly*, vol. 1, no. 2, pp. 165–73.

Committee of Inquiry into the United Kingdom Prison Services (1979) (The May Committee), Cmnd 7673 (London: HMSO).

Constable, M. (1974), *Report on Tied Accommodation* (London: Shelter).

Coser, L. A. (1974), *Greedy Institutions* (New York: Free Press).

Davidoff, L. (1979), 'The separation of home and work? Landladies and lodgers in nineteenth and twentieth century England', in *Fit Work for Women*, ed. S. Burman (London: Croom Helm), pp. 64–97.

Deem, R. (1981), 'Women, leisure and inequality', Paper presented to the Annual Conference of the British Sociological Association.

Delmar, R. (1976), 'Looking again at Engels' "Origins of the Family, Private Property and the State"', in *The Rights and Wrongs of Women*, ed. J. Mitchell and A. Oakley (Harmondsworth: Penguin), pp. 271–87.

Delphy, C. (1976), 'Continuities and discontinuities in marriage and divorce', in *Sexual Divisions and Society: Process and Change*, ed. D. L. Barker and S. Allen (London: Tavistock), pp. 76–89.

Delphy, C. (1977), *The Main Enemy: a materialist analysis of women's oppression*, Explorations in Feminism No. 3 (London: Women's Research and Resources Centre).

Delphy, C. (1980), 'A materialist feminism is possible', trans. D. Leonard, *Feminist Review*, no. 4, pp. 79–105.

Dennis, N., Henriques, F. and Slaughter, C. (1969), *Coal is Our Life*, 2nd edn (London: Tavistock).

Department of Employment (1980), *Family Expenditure Survey, Report for 1979* (London: HMSO).

Dobrofsky, L. R. and Batterson, C. T. (1977), 'The military wife and feminism', *Signs: Journal of Women in Culture and Society*, vol. 2, Spring, pp. 675–84.

Dubin, R. (1962), 'Industrial workers' worlds: a study of the "central life interests" of industrial workers', in *Human Behaviour and Social Processes*, ed. A. M. Rose (London: Routledge & Kegan Paul), pp. 227–66.

Dunnell, K. (1979), *Family Formation 1976*, Office of Population, Censuses and Surveys, Social Survey Division (London: HMSO).

Edgell, S. (1980), *Middle Class Couples: A Study of Segregation, Domination and Inequality in Marriage* (London: Allen & Unwin).

Edholm, F., Harris, O. and Young, K. (1977), 'Conceptualising women', *Critique of Anthropology*, vol. 9 and 10, no. 3, pp. 101–30.

Eichler, M. (1973), 'Women as personal dependents', in *Women in Canada*, ed. M. Stephenson (Toronto: New Press), pp. 36–55.

Eichler, M. (1980), *The Double Standard: A Feminist Critique of Feminist Social Science* (London: Croom Helm).

Eichler, M. (1981), 'Power, dependency, love and the sexual division of labour', *Women's Studies International Quarterly*, vol. 4, no. 2, pp. 201–19.

Elbert, S. and Glastonbury, M. (1978), *Inspiration and Drudgery: notes on literature and domestic labour in the nineteenth century*, Explorations in Feminism No. 5 (London: Women's Research and Resources Centre).

Engels, F. (1940), *The Origins of the Family, Private Property and the State* (London: Lawrence & Wishart).

Epstein, C. F. (1971a), 'Law partners and marital partners: strains and solutions in the dual-career family enterprise', *Human Relations*, vol. 24, no. 6, pp. 549–64.

Epstein, C. F. (1971b), *Woman's Place: Options and Limits in Professional Careers* (Berkley, Calif.: University of California Press).

Evans, J. L. (1965), 'Psychiatric illness in the physician's wife', *American Journal of Psychiatry*, vol. 122, pp. 159–63.

Farmer, M. (1970), *The Family* (London: Longman).

Farris, A. (1978), 'Commuting', in *Working Couples*, ed. R. Rapoport and R. N. Rapoport (London: Routledge & Kegan Paul), pp. 100–7.

Festing, S. (1977), *Fishermen* (London: David & Charles).

Finch, J. (1980), 'Devising conventional performances: the case of clergymen's wives', *Sociological Review*, vol. 28, no. 4, pp. 851–70.

Finch, J. and Groves, D. (1980), 'Community care and the family: a case for equal opportunities?', *Journal of Social Policy*, vol. 9, pt 4, pp. 487–511.

Flynch, C. H. and Davidoff, L. (1978), 'Introduction', in *Inspiration and Drudgery: notes on literature and domestic labour in the nineteenth century*, ed. S. Elbert and M. Glastonbury, Explorations in Feminism No. 5 (London: Women's Research and Resources Centre), pp. 1–9.

Fogarty, M., Rapoport, R. and Rapoport, R. N. (1971), *Sex, Career and Family* (London: Allen & Unwin).

Fowlkes, M. R. (1980). *Behind Every Successful Man: Wives of Medicine and Academe* (New York: Columbia University Press).

Frankenberg, R. (1976), 'In the production of their lives, men (?) . . . sex and gender in British community studies', in *Sexual Divisions and Society: Process and Change*, ed. D. L. Barker and S. Allen (London: Tavistock), pp. 25–51.

Friedson, E. (1970), *The Profession of Medicine* (New York: Dodd, Mead).

Gardiner, J. (1976), 'Political economy of domestic labour in capitalist society', in *Dependence and Exploitation in Work and Marriage*, ed. D. L. Barker and S. Allen (London: Longman), pp. 109–20.

Gavron, H. (1966), *The Captive Wife* (Harmondsworth: Penguin).

Gershuny, J. I. and Pahl, R. E. (1980), 'Britain in the decade of the three economics', *New Society*, vol. 51, no. 900, 3.1.80, pp. 7–9.

Gillespie, D. L. (1972), 'Who has the power? The marital struggle', in *Family, Marriage and the Struggle of the Sexes*, Recent Sociology No. 4 (New York: Macmillan), pp. 121–50.

Glastonbury, M. (1978), 'Holding the pens', in *Inspiration and Drudgery: notes on literature and domestic labour in the nineteenth century*, ed. S. Elbert and M. Glastonbury, Explorations in Feminism No. 5 (London: Women's Research and Resources Centre), pp. 27–46.

Goffman, E. (1961), 'The character of total institutions', in *A Sociological Reader on Complex Organisations*, ed. A. Etzioni (New York: Holt, Rinehart & Winston).

Goffman, E. (1963), *Stigma: Notes on the Management of Spoiled Identity* (Englewood Cliffs, NJ: Prentice-Hall).

Goffman, E. (1968), *Asylums* (Harmondsworth: Penguin, first pub. by Doubleday, 1961).

Goldman, N. (1973), 'Women in the armed forces', *American Journal of Sociology*, vol. 78, no. 4, pp. 892–911.

Gowler, D. and Legge, K. (1978), 'Hidden and open contracts in marriage', in *Working Couples*, ed. R. Rapoport and R. N. Rapoport (London: Routledge & Kegan Paul), pp. 47–61.

Gray, K. J. (1977), *The Reallocation of Property on Divorce* (Abingdon, Oxon.: Professional Books).

Groves, D. (forthcoming), *Women and Occupational Pensions*, Ph.D. thesis, University of London.

Haberstein, R. W. (1962), 'Sociology of occupations: the case of the American funeral director', in *Human Behaviour and Social Process,* ed. A. M. Rose (London: Routledge & Kegan Paul), pp. 225–46.

Hamill, L. (1976), *Wives as Sole and Joint Breadwinners*, Economic Advisers' Office, DHSS (London: HMSO).

Hanmer, J. (1977), 'Violence and the social control of women', in *Power and the State*, ed. G. Littlejohn, B. Smart, J. Wakeford and N. Yuval-Davis (London: Croom Helm), pp. 217–38.

Harari, E. (1981), 'Pathological grief in doctors' wives', *British Medical Journal*, vol. 282, 3.1.81, pp. 33–4.

Harris, C. C. (1969), *The Family* (London: Allen & Unwin).

Harris, C. C. (1977), 'Changing conceptions of the relation between the family and societal form in western society', in *Industrial Society: Class, Cleavage and Control*, ed. R. Scase (London: Allen & Unwin), pp. 74–89.

Himmelweit, S. and Mohun, S. (1977), 'Domestic labour and capital', *Cambridge Journal of Economics*, vol. 1, no. 1, pp. 15–32.

Hollowell, P. G. (1968), *The Lorry Driver* (London: Routledge & Kegan Paul).

Hope, E., Kennedy, M. and de Winter, A. (1976), 'Homeworkers in north London', in *Dependence and Exploitation in Work and Marriage*, ed. D. L. Barker and S. Allen (London: Longman), pp. 88–108.

Horobin, F. and McIntosh, J. (1977), 'Responsibility in general practice', in *Health and the Division of Labour*, ed. M. Stacey, M. Reid, C. Heath and R. Dingwall (London: Croom Helm), pp. 88–114.

Hughes, E. C. (1958), *Men and their Work* (New York: Free Press).

Hughes, E. C. (1959), 'The study of occupations', in *Sociology Today: Problems and Prospects*, ed. R. K. Merton, L. Bloom and L. S. Cottrell (New York: Basic Books), pp. 442–58.

Hughes, H. (1973), 'Maid of all work or departmental sister-in-law?', *American Journal of Sociology*, vol. 78, no. 4, pp. 767–72.

Hunt, P. (1980), *Gender and Class Consciousness* (London: Macmillan).

Jay, M. (1977), Interview broadcast on BBC Woman's Hour, 8.11.77.

Jones, B. (1970), 'The dynamics of marriage and motherhood', in *Sisterhood is Powerful*, ed. R. Morgan (New York: Vintage Books), pp. 46–61.

Kohl, S. B. (1977), 'Women's participation in the North American family form', *Women's Studies International Quarterly*, vol. 1 no. 1, pp. 47–54.

Komarovsky, M. (1967), *Blue Collar Marriage* (New York: Vintage Books).

Krause, E. A. (1971), *The Sociology of Occupations* (Boston, Mass.: Little, Brown).

Kuhn, A. (1978), 'Structures of patriarchy and capital in the family', in *Feminism and Materialism*, ed. A. Kuhn and A. M. Wolpe (London: Routledge & Kegan Paul, pp. 42–67).

Land, H. (1975), 'The myth of the male breadwinner', *New Society*, vol. 34, no. 679, 9.10.75, pp. 71–3.

Land, H. (1976), 'Women: supporters or supported?', in *Sexual Divisions and Society: Process and Change*, ed. D. L. Barker and S. Allen (London: Tavistock), pp. 108–32.

Land, H. (1978), 'Who cares for the family?', *Journal of Social Policy*, vol. 7, Pt 3, pp. 257–84.

Land, H. (1980), 'The family wage', *Feminist Review*, no. 6, pp. 55–78.

Lasch, C. (1977), *Haven in a Heartless World* (New York: Basic Books).

Leonard, D. (1980), *Sex and Generation: A Study of Courtship and Weddings* (London: Tavistock).

Lopata, H. Z. (1971), *Occupation Housewife* (London: OUP).

Lukes, S. (1973), *Emile Durkheim, his Life and Work: An Historical Study* (London: Allen Lane).

McIntosh, M. (1978), 'The state and the oppression of women', in *Feminism and Materialism*, ed. A. Kuhn and A. M. Wolpe (London: Routledge & Kegan Paul, pp. 254–89).

McIntosh, M. (1979), 'The welfare state and the needs of the dependent family', in *Fit Work for Women*, ed. S. Burman (London: Croom Helm), pp. 153–72.

Mackintosh, M. M. (1979), 'Domestic labour and the household', in *Fit Work for Women*, ed. S. Burman (London: Croom Helm), pp. 173–91.

Macintyre, S. (1978), 'Some notes on record-taking in an ante-natal clinic', *Sociological Review*, vol. 26, no. 3, pp. 595–611.

Mackie, L. and Patullo, P. (1977), *Women at Work* (London: Tavistock).

McLeod, K. (1976), *Wives of Downing Street* (London: Collins).

McPherson, M. (1975), *The Power Lovers: An Intimate Look at Politicians and Marriage* (New York: Putnam).

Marceau, J. (1976), 'Marriage, role division and social cohesion: the case of some French upper-middle class families', in *Dependence and Exploitation in Work and Marriage*, ed. D. L. Barker and S. Allen (London: Longman), pp. 204–23.

Marsh, A. (1979), *Women and Shiftwork*, Office of Population, Censuses and Surveys, Social Survey Division (London: HMSO).

Middleton, C. (1974), 'Sexual inequality and stratification theory', in *The Social Analysis of Class Structure*, ed. F. Parkin (London: Tavistock), pp. 179–203.

Ministry of Defence (1974), *Report of the Naval Welfare Committee* (London: HMSO).

Ministry of Defence (1976), *Report of the Army Welfare Inquiry Committee* (London: HMSO).

Mitchell, J. (1979), *Woman's Estate* (Harmondsworth: Penguin).

Mitchell, S. (1975), 'The policeman's wife – urban and rural', *The Police Journal*, vol. 48, pp. 79–88.

Moorhouse, G. (1977), *The Diplomats: The Foreign Office Today* (London: Cape).

Morgan, D. H. J. (1975), *Social Theory and the Family* (London: Routledge & Kegan Paul).

Morris, P. (1963), 'Staff problems in a maximum security prison', *Prison Service Journal*, vol. II, no. 6, pp. 3–15.

Mortimer, J., Hall, R. and Hill, R. (1978), 'Husbands' occupational attributes and constraints on wives' employment', *Sociology of Work and Occupations*, vol. 5, no. 3, pp. 285–313.

Moss, P. and Fonda, N. (1980), *Work and the Family* (London: Temple Smith).

Newby, H., Bell, C., Rose, G. and Saunders, P. (1978), *Property, Paternalism and Power* (London: Hutchinson).

Nicholson, P. J. (1980), *Goodbye Sailor: The Importance of Friendship in Family Mobility and Separation* (Inverness: Northpress).

Normàn-Butler, B. (1972), *Victorian Aspirations: The Life and Labour of Charles and Mary Booth* (London: Allen & Unwin).

Oakley, A. (1974a), *Housewife* (Harmondsworth: Penguin).

Oakley, A. (1974b), *The Sociology of Housework* (London: Martin Robertson).

Oakley, A. (1979), *Becoming a Mother* (London: Martin Robertson).

Oakley, A. and Oakley, R. (1979), 'Sexism in official statistics', in *Demystifying Social Statistics*, ed. J. Irvine, I. Miles and J. Evans (London: Pluto Press).

O'Donovan, K. (1979), 'The male appendage – legal definitions of women', in *Fit Work for Women,* ed. S. Burman (London: Croom Helm), pp. 134–52.

Owne, T. (1980), 'The wrong side of the tracks', *Low Pay Unit Pamphlet No. 14* (London: Low Pay Unit).

Pahl, J. (1980), 'Patterns of money management within marriage', *Journal of Social Policy*, vol. 9, pt 3, pp. 313–35.

Pahl, J. M. and Pahl, R. E. (1971), *Managers and their Wives* (Harmondsworth: Penguin).

Pahl, R. E. (1980), 'Employment, work and the domestic division of labour', *International Journal of Urban and Regional Research*, vol. 4, no. 1, pp. 1–20.

Papanek, H. (1973), 'Men, women and work: reflections on the two-person career', *American Journal of Sociology*, vol. 78, no. 4, pp. 852–72.

Parker, S. (1973), 'Relations between work and leisure', in *Leisure and Society in Britain*, ed. M. A. Smith, S. Parker and C. S. Smith (London: Allen Lane), pp. 75–85.

Parsons, T. (1970), 'The normal American family', in *Marriage and the Family*, ed. M. Barash and A. Scourby (New York: Random House), pp. 193–210.

Peelo, M. (1971), 'More ardua than astra', *SAAFA Magazine*, October, pp. 9–10.

Philpot, T. (1980), 'A social worker with connections', *Community Care*, no. 325, 4.9.80, pp. 24–6.

Platt, J. (1976), *The Realities of Social Research* (London: University of Sussex Press).

Poloma, M. and Garland, T. N. (1971), 'The myth of the egalitarian family: familial roles and the professionally employed wife', in *The Professional Woman*, ed. A. Theodore (Cambridge, Mass.: Schenkman).

Porter, M. (1978), 'Consciousness and secondhand experience: wives and husbands in industrial action', *Sociological Review*, vol. 26, no. 2, pp. 263–82.

Purcell, K. (1978), 'Working women, women's work and the occupational sociology of being a woman', *Women's Studies International Quarterly*, vol. 1, no. 2, pp. 153–63.

Purcell, K. (1979), 'Militancy and acquiescence among women workers', in *Fit Work for Women,* ed. S. Burman (London: Croom Helm), pp. 122–33.

Purcell, K. (1981), 'Men wouldn't stand for it', Paper presented to the Annual Conference of the British Sociological Association.

Rapoport, R. and Rapoport, R. N. (1969), 'Work and family in contemporary society', in *The Family and Change*, ed. J. N. Edwards (New York: Knopf), pp. 385–408.

Rapoport, R. and Rapoport, R. N. (1971), *Dual Career Families* (Harmondsworth: Penguin).

Rapoport, R. and Rapoport, R. N. (1976), *Dual Career Families Re-examined* (London: Martin Robertson).

Rapoport, R. and Rapoport, R. N. (eds) (1978), *Working Couples* (London: Routledge & Kegan Paul).

Robinson, P. J. (1980), *Goodbye Sailor: The Importance of Friendship in Family Mobility and Separation* (Inverness: Northpress).

Rossi, A. (1971), 'Women in science: why so few?', in *The Other Half: Roads to Women's Equality,* ed. C. F. Epstein and W. J. Goode (Englewood Cliffs, NJ: Prentice-Hall), pp. 110–21.

Roth, J. (1963), *Timetables: Structuring the Passage of Time in Hospital Treatment and Other Careers* (New York: Bobbs-Merrill).

Rushton, P. (1979), 'Marxism, domestic labour and the capitalist economy', in *The Sociology of the Family*, Sociological Review Monograph No. 28 (Keele: University of Keele), pp. 32–48.

Russell, D. (1980), *The Tamarisk Tree: Vol. 2. My School and the Years of the War* (London: Virago).

Rutter, M. (1972), *Maternal Deprivation Reassessed* (Harmondsworth: Penguin).

Safilios-Rothschild, C. (1976), 'Dual linkages between occupational and family systems: a macro sociological analysis', in *Women and the Workplace*, ed. M. Blaxall and B. Reagan (Chicago: University of Chicago Press), pp. 51–60.

Salaman, G. (1971a), 'Some sociological determinants of occupational communities', *Sociological Review*, vol. 19, pp. 53–75.

Salaman, G. (1971b), 'Two occupational communities: examples of a remarkable convergence of work and non-work', *Sociological Review*, vol. 19, pp. 389–407.

Scase, R. and Goffee, R. (1980a), *The Real World of the Small Business Owner* (London: Croom Helm).

Scase, R. and Goffee, R. (1980b), 'Homelife in a small business', *New Society*, 30.10.80, pp. 220–2.

Secombe, W. (1974), 'The housewife and her labour under capitalism', *New Left Review*, no. 83, pp. 3–24.

Seidenberg, R. (1973), *Corporate Wives – Corporate Casualties?* (New York: Amacom).

Shimmin, S., McNally, J. and Liff, S. (1981), 'Pressures on women engaged in factory work', *Employment Gazette*, vol. 89, no. 8, pp. 344–9.

Smith, D. (1973), 'Women, the family and corporate capitalism', in *Women in Canada*, ed. M. L. Stephenson (Toronto: New Press), pp. 5–35.

Snell, M. (1979), 'Equal Pay and Sex Discrimination Acts: their impact in the workplace', *Feminist Review*, vol. 1, pp. 37–57.

Spedding, J. V. (1975), *Wives of the Clergy*, unpublished Ph.D. thesis, University of Bradford.

Stacey, M. (1960), *Tradition and Change: A Study of Banbury* (Oxford: OUP).

Stacey, M. (1981), 'The division of labour revisited or overcoming the two Adams', in *Practice and Progress: British Sociology 1950–1980*, ed. P. Abrams, R. Deem, J. Finch and P. Rock (London: Allen & Unwin), pp. 172–90.

Stacey, M., Batstone, E., Bell, C. and Murcott, A. (1975), *Power, Persistence and Change: A Second Study of Banbury* (London: OUP).

Stacey, M. and Price, M. (1980), 'Women and power', *Feminist Review*, no. 5, pp. 33–52.

Strauss, A. L. and Becker, H. S. (1975), 'Careers, personality and adult socialisation', in *Professions, Work and Careers*, ed. A. L. Strauss (New Brunswick, NJ: Transaction Books), pp. 81–96.

Thompson, E. P. (1968), *The Making of the English Working Class* (Harmondsworth: Penguin).

Tunstall, J. (1962), *The Fishermen* (London: MacGibbon & Kee).

Tunstall, J. (1971), *Journalists at Work* (London: Constable).

Turner, C. (1971), 'Dual work households and marital dissolution', *Human Relations*, vol. 24, no. 6, pp. 535–48.

Voysey, M. (1975), *A Constant Burden: The Reconstitution of Family Life* (London: Routledge & Kegan Paul).

Wakeford, J. (1969), *The Cloistered Elite: A Sociological Analysis of the English Public Boarding School* (London: Macmillan).

Watson, W. (1964), 'Social mobility and social class in industrial communities', in *Closed Systems and Open Minds*, ed. M. Gluckman and E. Devour (London: Oliver & Boyd), pp. 129–56.

West, J. (1978), 'Women, sex and class', in *Feminism and Materialism*, ed. A. Kuhn and A. M. Wolpe (London: Routledge & Kegan Paul), pp. 220–53.

Westland, P. (1980), 'Back up your man', *Family Circle*, August 1980, pp. 86–8.

Whittaker, B. (1964), *The Police* (Harmondsworth: Penguin).

Whyte, W. H. (1971), 'The wife problem', in *The Other Half: Roads to*

Women's Equality, ed. C. F. Epstein and W. J. Goode (Englewood Clifts, NJ: Prentice-Hall), pp. 79–86.

Wilensky, H. L. (1961), 'Orderly careers and social participation: the impact of work history on social integration in the middle mass', *American Sociological Review*, vol. 26, no. 4, pp. 521–39.

Williams, W. M. (1969), *The Sociology of an English Village: Gosforth*, 2nd edn (London: Routledge & Kegan Paul).

Wilson, E. (1980), *Only Half Way to Paradise: Women in Postwar Britain 1945–1968* (London: Tavistock).

Wilson, M. (1976), 'Supporters' club', *New Statesman*, 13.8.76, p. 212.

Wrong, D. (1961), 'The oversocialised conception of man in modern sociology', *American Sociological Review*, vol. 26, no. 2, pp. 183–93.

Young, M. and Willmott, P. (1973), *The Symmetrical Family* (London: Routledge & Kegan Paul).

Zaretsky, E. (1976), *Capitalism, the Family and Personal Life* (London: Pluto Press).

Index